"I have known Tanya Holland for three decades. I have watched her grow from food enthusiast to accomplished chef and tastemaker to now a published authority on the cuisine she loves most. *California Soul* is a book that will live on my kitchen counter with drips of California olive oil and splats of buttermilk on every page. Who can possibly resist a Fried Artichoke Po' Boy?"

—Bobby Flay, chef, restaurateur, author, and food media host

"If there is a person who defines California Soul it is Chef Tanya Holland. Way deeper than an ethereal meaning of the word *soul*, she lives and breathes the lexicon of African American cuisine into her craft and this work of art. Get this book for the food but read it to feed your mind. From migration paths to highlighting iconic figures, she gives a platform to the diaspora in America and a voice to the inaudible."

—Kwame Onwuachi, James Beard Award–winning chef and author of *Notes from a Young Black Chef* and *My America*

"What a gift to have Tanya Holland bring us *California Soul*! Food is the story of movement, and this is a beautiful and timely contribution to the story of Black food culture in California."

—Stephen Satterfield, founder and editor of Whetstone and host of *High on the Hog*

W9-BWH-710

TANYA HOLLAND'S

CALIFORNIA
SOUL

TANYA HOLLAND'S

CALIFORNIA SOUL

Recipes *from a* Culinary Journey West

TANYA HOLLAND

with Maria C. Hunt *and* Dr. Kelley Fanto Deetz

Foreword by Alice Walker

Photographs by Aubrie Pick

TEN SPEED PRESS
California | New York

CONTENTS

FOREWORD
by *Alice Walker*

California Soul is the most beautiful cookbook I've ever read. Or seen. It is an unusually moving read, just for the stories, before you even get to a serious consideration of the food. Like any great book that is steeped in the love of its characters, California Soul is instructive and at the same time remarkably moving. Reading it I was constantly thinking: I may never make these great dishes, but I will reread this cookbook for years to come, for the stories of incredible gutsy, resourceful, intrepid, Black people who not only came West to California from the South to begin new lives, but continued living lives of bravery, will, creativity, and inspiration for generations, following their initial arrival here, and continuing to this day.

The photographs—of landscape, food, and people—are as compelling as the narrative. Evocative flowers, orchards, fields. The faces of people! So honest. So simple. So true. It is as if the black people in this book represent a basic character: that of honesty, steadfastness, determination, and . . . satisfaction. Each person, whether date farmer or apple grower, has chosen the path suited to herself or himself, has moved heaven and earth to fulfill a dream of growing food that will sustain others as well as themselves, and has achieved the peace of soul that comes from knowing one's self to be both irreplaceable, sui generis, and secure in one's own dream of what an abundant life can be.

Then there are the recipes. Wondrous creations, all. Each recipe is offered with a loving clarity that makes the reader hungry to try to make such a dish herself. Each recipe a creation of gustatory genius. Each recipe marvelous in its unexpected, often unusual, mixture of ingredients and inspiration. Almost every recipe connects us to hundreds of years and generations of black people, in our families and communities, who did for us whatever they could to make us realize we were loved. This so often involved offering us the best taste of their love through their food.

It will be a challenge to read this cookbook without shedding a tear. It is that radical. That profound. And it is so us! Whoever thought there'd be a cookbook some day that left us sobbing!? With thanksgiving. For it says: We have been fed all along by people who loved us. People who offered us the best, most creative offerings that they had. And generation after generation they never failed to remember to feed us well. With spirituality, with creativity, with dance, with prayer, song, and the foundation of all of these things: unforgettable food presented by great cooks and chefs who are grateful to acknowledge, cherish, and lift up the ancestors, by being exactly who they are.

INTRODUCTION

I am Black and I am African American. I use these terms interchangeably. Both are accurate descriptors. My skin is dark brown and my ancestors are from the African diaspora. I live in California and I am a Californian. I claim it all. Black belongs to the diaspora and African American is specific to my experience in the United States as a descendant of the enslaved people brought to this country from Africa by Europeans. Americans have been and still are all on the journey together. And as an African American woman, the contribution that my ancestors made to what Americans eat and how we eat is significant. No matter where we migrated from or ended up, our food comes with us and tells our story. I am contributing and this is my story. I have a California Soul.

I'm not from the South, but that's really where my family's story as I know it begins. My dad, Hollis, is from Virginia, and my mom, Annette, was born and raised in Louisiana. I spent many alternating summers visiting my grandparents in their respective homes. In Virginia, they raised chickens and vegetables. My Louisiana grandparents had a small vegetable garden with fruit trees, and my maternal grandfather had a little corner store that sold pickles, pralines, penny candy, and other goodies. Many of my grandparents' siblings left the South during the Great Migration, and most of my parents' siblings left as soon as they graduated from high school.

My parents met one summer in Oakland, and I like to think that destined my life to be there. Once married, my parents settled on the East Coast, where my dad attended college. I was born in Hartford, Connecticut, and I was just two years old when we moved to Rochester, New York, where he accepted a position as an industrial engineer with Eastman Kodak.

He and my mother found themselves building a life in this new city at the height of the Civil Rights era when reports about protests, marches, and riots across the country filled the nightly news broadcasts. At this same time, my parents founded The Gourmet Club, a dinner club they shared with five other couples, all ethnically and racially diverse friends and coworkers. Throughout this national upheaval, they were hosting and communing over food and beverages. Everyone cooked together and ate together. Everyone got along. I saw early on how sharing a meal could bring people together.

My parents were grateful for their new home, but they still longed for the family, friends, and familiar flavors they enjoyed in Louisiana and Virginia. They both cooked often, filling our home with tempting scents. My mother introduced her new friends to her gumbo, cornbread, and fried chicken.

My dad made home fries for breakfast, fried apples, and baked cakes from scratch, just like his mother. These foods satisfied their nostalgia for home and gave me a sensory connection to the South.

The Great Migration took all my maternal great-aunts and great-uncles to the West Coast. My great-aunts Lottie and Susie, left Shreveport, Louisiana, and started a restaurant in Portland, Oregon, in the 1940s. Lottie and Susie's Place had live music, and the kitchen never closed, so they served chicken dinners, barbecue, and chitlins anytime you wanted. It seems like chicken dinners and 24-7 hospitality run in my blood. Two of my other great-aunts landed in Southern California, and I still have distant cousins in the San Francisco Bay Area, where I planned to host the biannual family reunion in 2021, but obviously that was postponed!

For my first trip to California, my parents drove their green Chrysler Satellite Sebring cross-country to visit my great-aunt Vera, my maternal great-uncle's wife. She was a schoolteacher in Oakland, California, with a hairdresser side hustle that allowed her luxuries like an eye-catching Mercedes-Benz sedan. She was impressive in many ways and, standing nearly six feet tall, spoke with a deep East Texas drawl; she was as dark and savory as the roux she created for her signature gumbo. Aunt Vera was irreverent, a fierce multitasker, and easily our favorite auntie. I may have learned a thing or two from her.

Aunt Vera moved through her kitchen like a professional chef, cooking and tasting her dishes in progress and adjusting seasonings until the flavors met her standard. She'd draft anyone standing nearby as a prep cook, doling out commands softened only by her distinctive accent that still echoes in my ear.

After that first trip, many years went by before I returned to California. But the Golden State was always on my mind—especially during the winters in Brooklyn, New York, where I last lived on the East Coast. I went out to California in 2000 to visit friends and fell in love with the landscape, architecture, slower pace, and farm to table foodways. It struck me as a perfect destination for the next phase in my career and life. I booked a flight that departed September 18, 2001, to start my new life in the West. The devastation of 9/11 shook me but made me even more determined to go—and I've never looked back.

When I arrived in Oakland, I wanted to learn everything about my new home, especially Black history. I heard firsthand stories of African American pioneers from local docent Jerry Thompson, as well as by visiting the local bookstore Marcus Books and art galleries helmed by Samuel Fredericks and Joyce Gordon, all featuring Black artists and writers. In West Oakland, everyone had a story of railway porters and cowboys, the real Black Panther Party in Oakland, and progressive educators, doctors, and lawyers. These people were pioneers, and I felt like I had found my people and my place.

California offered an openness to ambitious (female and Black) thought leaders and entrepreneurs that I hadn't experienced on the East Coast. It seemed like a perfect place and time to start a new venture. I was teaching cooking classes, studying wine, and still taping my Food Network show, but I sorely missed working in restaurants. Before long, I found the right opportunity to open my own place.

Feeding people and bringing them together over food is my greatest passion, and I attended cooking school in France in the 1990s to pursue my dream of becoming a restaurateur. Plus, my family history was filled with resourceful, entrepreneurial Black women and men who used their skills, common sense, and intelligence to care for their families and improve their communities. The restaurant industry turned out to be the ideal place for me to create something unique. I began to build the culinary expertise and awareness I needed to attract investors, build a thriving business, care for my family, and nurture my newfound community.

Shortly after arriving in California, I catered for a family with three daughters. Even though the girls were aged twelve to sixteen, they asked detailed questions about whether the shrimp I was serving was wild-caught or farm-raised. Their curiosity and concern impressed me. Here in California, many people want to know and really care about where their food is sourced.

This is especially true in the Bay Area, thanks to influential Chez Panisse founder Alice Waters, who helped make seasonal eating a community value. She created the now ubiquitous farm-to-table experience. Here, people rarely eat tomatoes out of season, but instead shop at farmers' markets year-round and wait in long lines for the best artisan bread and ice cream.

Now I have developed close relationships with farmers, growers, breeders, bakers, and coffee roasters. Through these relationships, we have formed a network that has economic, social, and environmental power. As we learn from one another about new sources of ingredients and how to work with fresh, locally grown products, the canned or preserved forms have become a thing of the past. Now I use fresh, seasonal ingredients more than 90 percent of the time, and it has transformed my cooking.

At the same time, I noticed that Oakland had very few eating establishments representing the local Black culture in an elevated way. I wanted to honor my culinary heritage and the food I learned from my parents and aunties while highlighting the brilliant flavors of California's seasonal produce and local ingredients. Approaching food this way also let me live out my egalitarian values related to equity and sustainability. And I wanted to create a place where everyone felt welcome.

I realized these goals in 2008 when I opened my first location of Brown Sugar Kitchen on Martin Luther King's birthday on Mandela Parkway in the West Oakland neighborhood. Some of my regular customers included Ericka Huggins, one of the original founding members of the Black Panther Party. I'm grateful for how well the restaurant was received, but I'm more pleased with how my cooking continues to evolve. I'm continually looking for ways to support the food system's long-term viability and reduce its contribution to climate change and global warming.

When I moved the restaurant to the Uptown neighborhood in 2019, one of my guests, Paul Coates, former Black Panther and father of famed author Ta-Nehisi Coates, told me, "We travel all over this country, and you don't see any of us owning a place that looks like this. I know what it took for you to get here. Keep representing." That feedback felt like a gift. It's gratifying to share the space I've created with everyone looking for a little Southern and now Western hospitality.

These days I'm cooking more seasonal plant-based dishes and sustainable animal proteins and seek to source ingredients from the best food makers, including the Black winemakers, brewers, and farmers featured in this book. These modern Black culinary entrepreneurs are carrying on the legacy started by Black Southerners who moved to California, where they created a new way of eating and living.

I'm excited to share their stories and foodways through my podcast, television appearances, advocacy, and cookbooks. And I love traveling around the world sharing the food of my heritage through culinary diplomacy trips to Kazakhstan, Mexico, Singapore, China, and Japan, but . . . but my soul? My soul will always be anchored right here at home in California.

SPRING

Grilled Trinity Salad *with* Olive-Caper Dressing

Yield: 4 servings   **Prep time:** 25 minutes
Cook time: 15 minutes

Chopped onions, celery, and bell peppers make up the holy trinity of Cajun and Creole cooking, a foundational mixture similar to a French mirepoix. It is most often sautéed and used as the base of dishes like gumbo and jambalaya, but here, grilling the vegetables just until they are crisp-tender condenses their flavors.

Olive-Caper Dressing:
¼ cup red wine vinegar
1 tablespoon pitted finely chopped green olives, such as Castelvetrano
1 tablespoon pitted finely chopped black olives, such as Kalamata
1 tablespoon finely chopped fresh flat-leaf parsley
1 teaspoon chopped capers
½ cup extra-virgin olive oil
Salt and freshly ground black pepper

1 green bell pepper
1 red bell pepper
1 orange bell pepper
1 sweet onion, such as Vidalia, cut into ½-inch slices
3 celery stalks, trimmed
2 jalapeño chiles
2 tablespoons extra-virgin olive oil
Salt and freshly ground black pepper

To make the dressing:
In a bowl whisk together the vinegar, both olives, parsley, and capers. Slowly drizzle in the olive oil while whisking continuously, until the dressing is emulsified. Season with salt and black pepper. Set aside.

Place the whole bell peppers, onion, celery, and jalapeños on a large rimmed baking sheet. Drizzle with the olive oil, rubbing it all over the vegetables to lightly coat them. Sprinkle with salt and black pepper.

Prepare the grill for direct cooking over high heat (about 450°F). Brush the cooking grates clean. Place the vegetables on the grates and grill over high heat with the lid closed, turning them every so often. Grill the celery just until charred marks appear, about 2 minutes; cook the onion until marks appear and it starts to soften, about 4 minutes; and grill the peppers and jalapeños until they blacken all over, about 10 minutes. As each vegetable is ready, transfer it back to the baking sheet.

Place the bell peppers in a bowl and cover them with a plate to trap the steam. Let stand for 5 minutes, or until they're cool enough to handle. Remove the seeds, stems, cores, and membranes from the bell peppers and jalapeños. Peel away and discard the charred skins.

Cut the bell peppers lengthwise into ½-inch-wide strips. Roughly chop the onion and celery. Finely chop the jalapeños. Add all the vegetables to a bowl. Drizzle with some of the dressing, then season with salt and pepper. Serve with the remaining dressing passed alongside.

Westward Migration

Bridget "Biddy" Mason was one of the earliest African Americans to migrate from the Deep South to California. Born into slavery on a Mississippi plantation in 1818, Biddy's first thirty years were spent laboring at several plantations throughout Georgia, South Carolina, and Mississippi. In 1848, she and her three daughters walked 1,700 miles to Utah, following their enslaver and a three-hundred-wagon caravan. Biddy was responsible for cooking for the encampments, being a midwife, and herding the cattle. Her forced migration ended up taking the family to San Bernardino, California, where slavery was illegal. After meeting several free Black Californians, she sued her owner and won freedom for her family. Biddy then moved them to Los Angeles, bought land with money she earned as a midwife, and established what would become the oldest church founded by an African American in the city, now known as the First African Methodist Episcopal Church of Los Angeles. It is on Azusa Street, which became the first African American business district in L.A. Biddy's bravery, philanthropy, and entrepreneurship helped draw thousands of African American migrants to California.

Between 1916 and 1970, six million African Americans migrated out of Southern states into urban centers in the North and westward toward Washington, Oregon, and California during the Great Migration. Between 1850 and 1860, more than four thousand African Americans made their way to California, settling in Los Angeles, San Francisco, and Sacramento. Two large waves of western Black migration occurred between 1915 and 1918 due to the boll weevil infestations throughout the Southern agricultural communities and the employment opportunities created by World War I. Racism and the rise of the Ku Klux Klan also drove large waves of emigration as Jim Crow laws took hold throughout the southern US. Another wave came with the 1929 stock market crash. It surged higher at the start of World War II, as the war efforts created enticing economic opportunities in places like Los Angeles and Richmond, California. By 1930, more than 50,000 African Americans were residing in California's major cities, 338,000 more moved into the state during WWII, and by 1950, California's cities were home to almost a quarter of a million Black people.

This migration brought a sense of hope and determination to those leaving their roots in places like Louisiana, Texas, and Georgia. These westward migrants were searching for a new life, the American dream, and they quickly established distinct African American communities throughout California.

Creating a sense of cultural identity is one of the most important parts of settling in a new place. Black-owned businesses flourished in South Central Los Angeles, Watts, San Diego's Gaslamp Quarter, West Oakland, Richmond, and Sacramento. These enclaves were called everything from Harlem West to Bronzeville, and they became the foundation for what became California Soul food: individuals, restaurants, and grocers recreating Black Southern food in a new land.

Roasted Halibut *with* Green Beans *and* Sweet Potatoes

Yield: 4 servings   **Prep time:** 25 minutes
Cook time: 35 to 40 minutes

This flaky, rich white fish is a joy to cook with and makes a super-simple weeknight dinner that packs a lot of flavor. The garlic compound butter is delicious on any vegetable or fish. You could also make the butter in a food processor if chopping is not your thing. You may want to make a little extra butter and freeze it to use when you need a flavor pop for vegetables, fish, or crusty bread.

Garlic Compound Butter:
3 tablespoons unsalted
   or lightly salted butter,
   softened
1 garlic clove, minced
1 tablespoon minced shallot
1 tablespoon chopped
   fresh chives
Zest of 1 lemon

2 medium sweet potatoes,
   cut into wedges
¼ to ½ teaspoon cayenne
   pepper
½ teaspoon ground cumin
½ teaspoon ground coriander
1 teaspoon salt
1 tablespoon extra-virgin
   olive oil
1 pound green beans,
   ends trimmed
Salt
Four 6-ounce halibut fillets
Juice of 1 lemon
Chives for garnishing

Preheat the oven to 450°F.

To make the butter:
In a bowl, mix together the butter, garlic, shallot, chives, and the lemon zest. Set aside.

Place the sweet potatoes in a single layer on an 18 by 13-inch half-sheet pan. In a small bowl, combine the cayenne pepper, cumin, coriander, and salt and mix well. Drizzle the potatoes with olive oil and toss well with the spice mixture. Roast until the potatoes are almost fully tender and start to brown, 15 to 20 minutes.

Take the potatoes out of the oven and move them to one side of the pan, keeping them in a single layer. Arrange the green beans on the pan and top them with 2 teaspoons of the garlic butter. Sprinkle with salt and toss well. Return to the oven for 5 minutes.

Take the pan out of the oven and slide the green beans to the opposite side of the pan to create space for the halibut. Place the halibut fillets in a single layer in the center of the pan. Generously slather the halibut evenly with the remaining garlic butter. Return the pan to the oven and bake just until the halibut is cooked through, and the green beans are crisp-tender, 10 to 12 minutes.

Sprinkle the lemon juice and chives over the entire pan.

Seared Chicken Livers on Toasted Brioche *with* Cherries *and* Shallots

Yield: 4 servings   **Prep time:** 15 minutes
Cook time: 10 minutes

Like many people with parents from the South, I grew up eating fried chicken livers. My mother adored them, but I didn't care for them much then. But I love them now, and they remind me of her. Organ meats were sometimes seen as poor folks' food, but offal and homemade charcuterie have recently become more appreciated. The French have a long love affair with liver, and Cognac, shallots, and cherries elevate this humble protein. Serve them with endive, or as an appetizer on toasted brioche.

1 pound chicken livers
Salt and freshly ground
  pepper
1 tablespoon extra-virgin
  olive oil
2 tablespoons butter
1 shallot, thinly sliced
2 fresh sage leaves
15 cherries, halved and pitted
¼ cup brandy
1 tablespoon champagne
  vinegar
4 slices brioche, toasted

Pat the chicken livers dry with a paper towel. Remove any green areas and stringy connective tissue. Season the livers with salt and pepper.

Heat the olive oil and 1 tablespoon of the butter in a sauté pan over medium-high heat. When the pan is hot and the butter is melted, add the livers in a single layer, in batches if necessary, and sauté just until golden brown on the outside but still pink on the inside, about 45 seconds per side. Transfer the livers to a plate and set aside.

Add the remaining 1 tablespoon butter to the pan with the shallot and sage, sprinkle with salt, and cook until the shallot is softened and just starting to brown, about 4 minutes. Add the cherries and cook for 1 minute, to slightly soften them. Remove the pan from the heat and carefully add the brandy. Return the pan to the heat and cook, scraping the bottom of the pan, until the brandy is reduced by half. Add the champagne vinegar and stir. Remove from the heat and add the chicken livers back to the pan just until warmed through.

Place the livers on the brioche and top with the cherry and shallot mixture.

Sam Cobb *of* Sam Cobb Farms *in Desert Hot Springs*

Sam Cobb says he was three when he fell in love with tractors. He couldn't wait to drive one of those shiny green John Deeres with the golden-yellow wheels.

Today, Cobb and his wife Maxine run Sam Cobb Farms, where they produce Deglet Noor, Bahri, and Black Gold dates on seventy-five acres in the arid southern California desert.

Growing up on Annadale Avenue in Fresno just across the street from fields, he always ran to the window to see the tractors go by. By the age of four, he was on the porch. By age five, he was across the street on the edge of the field. He was six when a Black farmer named Ralph Dillingham gave him his first tractor ride. "I was in heaven," Cobb says. "I still wear a John Deere hat every day. Some people think I'm advertising a product. I'm reliving my childhood."

From age six to eleven, Cobb worked with Dillingham, earning bubblegum, hamburgers, and skills that he still uses today. His parents, who left the Mississippi Delta in 1948 to give the family a better life, didn't understand. "My parents told me, 'Don't have anything to do with the field,'" he says. "Everybody said, 'You're crazy. We just got out of the field. And you want to go back?'"

Cobb didn't care. In high school, he was the only Black kid in the Future Farmers of America club. "More than anything, I really wanted to be a classic corn farmer and drive a tractor and have the equipment," Cobb says.

So, he studied agriculture science in college. Armed with knowledge about irrigation, fertilizers, plant nutrition, and pesticides, he started farming green beans, peppers, turnips, and casaba melons. Even though he was educated, that didn't keep his first foray into farming from going belly-up in 1987. He realized that the economics didn't work; the margin between wholesale and retail was his profit.

He started working for the USDA, visiting California farmers and helping them with advice or loans. All the while, he was plotting his return to farm life. In 1996, Cobb was transferred to Indio near Palm Springs to support local date farmers. He saw how well they were doing financially, and he "fell in love with dates" in 1996.

Dates are a tree crop that yield what you might call compounding interest, in the form of more date trees. Cobb explains that when you plant one date tree, in seven years, it will send up shoots that will become seven more trees. He worked out a plan: Plant a hundred trees across five acres, and in seven years, he'd have seven hundred trees. "The USDA woman's eyes lit up," he says, and "I started convincing myself." He and his wife sold their house in La Quinta, bought a hundred trees, installed irrigation, and started waiting.

They grow and sell the dates directly to consumers online and from their farm stand. His pride and joy is the Black Gold, an exclusive variety that Cobb developed. The fruits are dark-skinned on the outside and golden-fleshed inside with two textures, as well as the flavors of caramel, dark chocolate, and cherry.

Cobb can tell you just about anything about dates except how to cook with them. "I'm a date eater, but I don't come up with recipes," he says.

Homemade Benne Seed Olive Oil Crackers *with* Black-Eyed Pea Dip

Yield: 32 crackers and 2 cups dip
Prep time: Overnight soak for the peas, plus 30 minutes for the crackers
Cook time: 40 minutes for the peas, plus 15 minutes for the crackers

Black-eyed peas deserve to be eaten way more often than just on New Year's Day. And a soul food meal, restaurant, or menu without black-eyed peas is missing some of its soul.

Black-Eyed Pea Dip:
¾ cup dried black-eyed peas
3 tablespoons neutral oil, such as grapeseed
2 tablespoons white wine vinegar
2 garlic cloves
2 teaspoons grated fresh ginger
2 teaspoons fresh thyme
1 teaspoon onion powder
1 teaspoon smoked paprika
Kosher salt

Crackers:
1 cup all-purpose flour
½ teaspoon fine sea salt
¼ cup water, plus 1 tablespoon
3 tablespoons extra-virgin olive oil
3 tablespoons benne (sesame) seeds
Flaky sea salt, such as Maldon

To make the dip:
Soak the peas in cold water overnight. Drain, add them to a pot, cover with water, place over medium-high heat, and let simmer until tender, about 40 minutes. Reserve ¼ cup of the cooking liquid and drain. Add all but ¼ cup of the cooked peas to a food processor. Add the oil, vinegar, garlic, ginger, thyme, onion powder, paprika, and 1 tablespoon of the reserved cooking water and puree until smooth. Add additional cooking water as necessary to thin to the desired consistency. Season with kosher salt. Transfer the dip to a bowl and gently stir in the remaining ¼ cup black-eyed peas.

To make the crackers:
Preheat the oven to 350°F.

In a bowl, whisk together the flour and sea salt. Stir in the ¼ cup water, olive oil, and 2 tablespoons of the benne seeds and mix just until a thick dough is formed. Lay out a silicone mat or a piece of parchment paper measuring 11½ by 16½ inches. Place the dough on the mat or parchment paper and flatten into a rectangle. Roll out the dough as thinly as possible until it covers the entire surface of the mat or parchment paper; it should be very thin. Using a pizza cutter, carefully cut the dough into thirty-two squares (eight by four). Lightly brush the dough with the remaining 1 tablespoon water and sprinkle with the remaining 1 tablespoon benne seeds and flaky sea salt.

Slide the parchment paper with the dough onto a baking sheet. Bake until the crackers turn lightly golden brown around the edges, 15 to 20 minutes. Let cool and serve with the dip.

Gumbo Z'herbes *with* Dungeness Crab *and* Prawns

Yield: 4 servings   **Prep time:** 20 minutes
Cook time: 55 minutes

Most people equate gumbo with New Orleans, but my mother is from Shreveport, and she and her sisters all make their own versions. My go-to gumbo is based on my mother's recipe, but I love making this vegetable-forward gumbo that New Orleans culinary icon Leah Chase made famous.

3 tablespoons vegetable oil
1 yellow onion, diced
2 shallots, minced
3 garlic cloves, minced
1 jalapeño chile, seeded and
  finely chopped
8 ounces fresh spinach
1 bunch fresh kale, large
  stems removed
2 cups vegetable stock, fish
  stock, or clam juice
One 14-ounce can coconut
  milk
1½ cups water
1 pound fresh or frozen okra,
  cut into ¼-inch pieces
1 tablespoon filé powder
1 tablespoon chopped
  fresh thyme
3 medium Yukon Gold or
  other yellow potatoes, diced
½ pound Dungeness crab
  meat, cleaned
1 pound head-on prawns or
  shrimp, peeled and deveined
Salt and freshly ground pepper
Cooked white rice for serving
Lemon slices for garnishing

In a large soup pot, heat the vegetable oil and cook the onion, shallots, garlic, and jalapeño over medium heat until soft, about 10 minutes. Add the spinach, kale, stock, coconut milk, and water and let simmer for 10 minutes, until the kale is wilted. Transfer the greens and 1 cup of the broth to a blender or food processor and puree. Return the greens mixture to the pot and add the okra, filé powder, thyme, and potatoes. Let simmer for about 15 minutes, until the potatoes are tender. Add the seafood. Continue cooking for 10 minutes, until the prawns are pink and the potatoes are soft. Season with salt and pepper.

To serve, spoon the rice into shallow bowls, and ladle the gumbo over the rice. Garnish with lemon slices.

Steamed Asparagus *with* Parsley Aioli

Yield: 8 servings   **Prep time:** 20 minutes
Cook time: 5 minutes

No matter what's going on with the weather, when I see the first asparagus at the farmers' market, I know spring is coming. It can be a long season lasting into mid-summer depending on the weather and the growing region. Green asparagus has a distinctive flavor that's one of the culinary hallmarks of spring, and a nice snap when you cook it just right. White asparagus, which is grown underground or in a dark space to prevent it from turning green, is super-sweet and juicy but a little more fibrous. Both types of asparagus are equally delicious with this bright green parsley aioli.

Parsley Aioli:
2 egg yolks
1 garlic clove, minced
1 teaspoon lemon zest
2 to 3 tablespoons lemon juice
½ cup neutral oil, such as grapeseed
3 tablespoons extra-virgin olive oil
½ teaspoon sea salt, plus more to taste
¼ teaspoon freshly ground pepper
½ cup chopped flat-leaf parsley

2½ pounds green or white asparagus
Ice water for chilling

To make the aioli:
In a blender or food processor, combine the egg yolks, garlic, lemon zest, and 2 tablespoons of the lemon juice and whirl until smooth. In a liquid measuring cup, combine the neutral and olive oils. With the blender running, slowly drizzle in the oils in a very thin stream until completely combined and the mixture turns thick, about 2 minutes. Add the salt, pepper, and parsley and pulse to blend. Taste and adjust the seasonings, adding more lemon juice if needed.

To make the asparagus:
Trim ½ to 1 inch from the asparagus ends. Cut a small slice from a trimmed end and taste; if the skin is fibrous, peel the stalks with a vegetable peeler and lay them flat on a cutting board. Bring a large saucepan of water to a simmer. Add the asparagus and let simmer covered until tender, 3 to 5 minutes (white asparagus may take longer). Transfer to a bowl of ice water, let cool, and then drain.

Serve the asparagus spears on a large platter with the aioli spooned over them, or on the side.

Sacramento

Sacramento is a city born out of the Gold Rush. Gold was discovered in 1848, igniting one of the largest migrations in American history. African Americans, some of whom were brought by their enslavers, began moving west to California. The United States census of 1849 listed 962 "free colored" people residing in California, and 240 of these people were in Sacramento.

The African American community in Sacramento was supported by Black churches. Both St. Andrew's African Methodist Episcopal Church, founded in 1850, and Siloam Baptist Church, founded in 1856, provided instant community to new residents. Black churches were essential in helping anchor new African American migrants to the developing neighborhoods. Sacramento was also home to many distinguished activists like Daniel Blue, a free man who went to court to liberate a young girl from her abusive enslaver. Blue won in a courtroom where he could not legally testify, only provide witnesses. Elizabeth Thorn Scott Flood was an educator who fought for equal education rights for all children, and Reverend Jeremiah Burke Sanderson opened Sacramento's first Black public school in 1856.

When Sacramento became the state capitol in 1854, the local African American community was at the forefront of the civil rights struggle in California, working alongside Chinese residents, who also faced brutality and racism. Multiple churches, schools, and organizations were established by the mid- to late 1800s. One of the most notable Black organizations was the armed militia known as the Sacramento Zouaves.

They were established in 1867 as a paramilitary group, and while they didn't serve in active duty, they engaged in local politics and helped encourage African Americans to get involved in the political process. The Zouaves' first sergeant, Robert Fletcher, led the militia to accompany President Ulysses S. Grant in a parade down K Street during Grant's 1879 visit to Sacramento.

In 1861, more than a third of African Americans in Sacramento worked in the food industry. As the Great Migration ramped up, Sacramento became a destination, and Southerners brought soul food to the West Coast. By the 1930s, "Harlem West" cities were popping up across California. Black entrepreneur George T. Dunlap opened Dunlap's Dining Room in 1930. Dunlap's never had a paper menu, and diners could choose from three options: fried chicken, baked ham, and T-bone steak. Dunlap's was listed on the National Register of Historic Places before it closed in 1968 when George Dunlap retired. The Eureka Club on Fourth and K was also an African American–owned institution, considered one of the largest jazz clubs in Northern California and was even promoted in a 1939 guide to white tourists attending the California Centennial.

For almost a century, African American settlers established significant businesses in Sacramento, especially in its West End neighborhood. One of them was the Hotel Clayton, which opened its doors in 1911 and then was later renamed the Marshall Hotel. The Clayton Club on the ground floor hosted many notable jazz performers, including Billie Holiday, Louis Armstrong, and Cab Calloway. Additionally, clubs like the MoMo, the Cotton Club, the Congo Club, and Zanzibar hosted stars such as Dizzy Gillespie, Louis Armstrong, and Cab Calloway.

Sweet Potato Buttermilk Pull-Apart Rolls

Yield: 15 rolls   **Prep time:** 45 minutes plus 3 hours to rise and cool
Cook time: 40 minutes

The sweet potato is a Southern staple that's closely related to the West African yam. It's a quintessential soul food ingredient that adds natural sweetness and color to any recipe. The tuber's own sugars mixed with the buttermilk's acidity give these buttery rolls a subtle balance of sweet and sour flavor that will bring joy to any dinner table.

1 small orange-fleshed sweet potato (6 ounces), peeled and cut into 1-inch chunks
Salt
½ cup buttermilk
¼ cup unsalted butter, at room temperature, plus about 3 tablespoons melted for brushing the rolls
4 cups all-purpose flour, plus more if needed
1 envelope instant yeast (2¼ teaspoons)
2 tablespoons granulated sugar
2 eggs

In a small saucepan, combine the sweet potato with enough water to cover. Add 1 teaspoon salt. Bring to a boil over high heat, then turn down the heat to medium and gently boil until the potato is very tender when pierced with a knife, 10 to 13 minutes.

Drain and transfer the potato to a mixing bowl. Mash with a potato masher or fork. Add the buttermilk and ¼ cup of the butter.

If you're using a stand mixer, beat the potato mixture in a bowl with a paddle attachment at medium-low speed until the mixture is fairly smooth, about 5 minutes. Add the flour, yeast, sugar, eggs, and 1½ teaspoons salt and mix on medium-low speed, scraping the bottom and sides of the bowl as needed with a spatula, until the dough is smooth and sticky and pulls away from the side of the bowl, about 8 minutes. Add a little more flour if the dough is very sticky.

If you're using a whisk, beat the potato mixture in a bowl with a whisk until the mixture is smooth and no lumps remain. Add the flour, yeast, sugar, eggs, and 1½ teaspoons salt and stir with a wooden spoon until the ingredients are well combined. Dump the dough onto a lightly floured work surface and knead until it becomes smooth and elastic, about 8 minutes; it will be slightly sticky.

Grease the insides of a clean bowl with butter. Transfer the dough to the bowl. Cover and let the dough rise in a warm, draft-free spot for about 1½ hours, or until it has more than doubled in size.

continued

Place the dough on a clean, ungreased surface and divide it into fifteen equal pieces (a kitchen scale works well here). One at a time, cup each piece of dough beneath your palm and work in quick, circular motions to form a tight ball, with only a tiny seam along the bottom. Grease a 9 by 13-inch baking pan with more butter and arrange the dough balls in evenly spaced rows. Brush the balls with butter, loosely cover the pan, and set aside in a warm place until the balls have turned puffy, doubled in size, and fill the pan, about 1 hour.

About 15 minutes before the rolls are done rising, preheat the oven to 375°F. Bake until golden brown, 15 to 20 minutes. Transfer the pan to a wire rack. Brush the rolls gently with a little butter. Let cool for 10 minutes, and then turn out the rolls onto the rack and invert again so they are bottom-side down. Let cool for about 20 minutes before serving.

Deviled Eggs *with* Andouille Sausage *and* Pickled Okra

Yield: 24 eggs, serves 8 to 12
Prep time: 20 minutes, plus at least 2 hours for the pickled okra to sit
Cook time: 25 minutes

The layers of textures, from the creamy yolk to the crisp scallions, as well as the andouille sausage—a New Orleans staple—and that hit of pickled okra, make these little devils quite fantastic. And you'll find lots of uses for the pickled okra (Bloody Marys, anyone?).

Pickled Okra:
12 ounces fresh small okra pods
1 Fresno or mildly spicy red chile
1½ cups apple cider vinegar
1 cup water
4 garlic cloves, sliced
⅓ cup granulated sugar
1 tablespoon salt
2 teaspoons black peppercorns
2 teaspoons mustard seeds

12 eggs
Ice water for chilling
¼ cup mayonnaise
2 tablespoons Dijon mustard
2 tablespoons chopped Pickled Okra (about 2 pods)
2 teaspoons okra pickling liquid
1 teaspoon Louisiana-style hot sauce, such as Crystal
3 ounces andouille sausage, diced small (about ¾ cup)
Salt and freshly ground pepper
2 scallions, thinly sliced, for garnishing

To make the pickled okra:
Clean two 1-pint jars. Trim any long okra stems and place the pods, alternating stem-side up and stem-side down, in the jars. Slice the chile in half lengthwise and put one half in each jar. For less spicy okra, remove the seeds from the chile. In a small saucepan, combine the vinegar, water, garlic, sugar, salt, peppercorns, and mustard seeds and bring to a simmer over low heat. Cook until the sugar and salt are dissolved, 7 to 8 minutes. Pour the mixture over the okra. Seal the jars and cool. Refrigerate for at least 2 hours before using. The pickled okra will keep in the fridge for up to 1 month.

To make the deviled eggs:
Bring a saucepan of water to a boil. Gently lower the eggs into the boiling water and bring back to a gentle simmer. Cook the eggs for 4 minutes. Turn off the heat, cover the pot, and let sit for 14 minutes. Drain the eggs and place them in ice water until cool. Once cooled, peel the eggs and halve lengthwise. Remove the yolks and place them in a bowl. Add the mayonnaise, mustard, pickled okra, okra pickling liquid, and hot sauce and mash until smooth.

In a sauté pan, cook the andouille sausage over medium heat until browned and crisp, about 5 minutes. Reserve 2 tablespoons of the andouille. Add the remaining andouille and any fat to the egg yolk mixture and mix to combine. Season the mixture with salt and pepper and transfer to a piping bag or a resealable plastic bag with the end snipped off. Pipe the mixture into the egg halves. Top with the reserved andouille and scallions.

Skillet Frittata *with* Bacon *and* Spring Onions

Yield: 4 to 6 servings   **Prep time:** 15 minutes
Cook time: 30 minutes

If you're in a hurry and want to impress your guests, whip up this frittata! Simplicity is the key here, and it's all about proportions. This is a dish that you can make at the last minute, but it looks and tastes like you put in the time. I love serving this frittata for brunch or a light supper along with fresh fruit or a green salad, and an aromatic white wine. The better the bacon, the better the frittata. I love using my dear friends Duskie and John Stewart-Estes's Black Pig Bacon.

6 slices bacon, chopped
1 cup thinly sliced
   spring onions, white
   and green parts
Salt and freshly ground
   pepper
8 eggs
⅓ cup sour cream
1 cup grated sharp white
   Cheddar cheese

Preheat the oven to 350°F.

Cook the bacon in a 10-inch cast-iron skillet over medium-high heat until well browned, about 8 minutes. Transfer the bacon with a slotted spoon to paper towels to drain. Reserve 2 tablespoons of the bacon fat from the pan and discard or save the rest for another use. Return 1 tablespoon of the bacon fat to the pan, and add the spring onions, season with salt and pepper, and cook just until the onions turn tender, about 1 minute. Transfer the onions from the pan and set aside with the bacon.

In a bowl, whisk together the eggs and sour cream and lightly season with salt and pepper. Stir in the Cheddar cheese until well combined.

Add the remaining reserved 1 tablespoon bacon fat to the pan over low heat. Pour in the egg-cheese mixture, making sure the cheese is evenly distributed. Sprinkle the bacon and onions evenly over the eggs and cook, without stirring, until you can see the frittata's edges start to set, 2 to 3 minutes. Place the pan in the oven and cook until the entire frittata is set but still just slightly jiggles in the center, 15 to 20 minutes. Remove from the oven and let sit for 5 minutes. Serve the frittata directly out of the pan, or invert it onto a platter or cutting board, then cut into wedges.

Fried Artichoke Po' Boy

Yield: 4 servings   **Prep time:** 1 hour
Cook time: 6 minutes

This po' boy is the vegetarian cousin of the classic sandwich you find all over its hometown of New Orleans. Traditional po' boys are filled with fried shrimp, oysters, or some sort of meat. This version swaps out the meat for fried artichokes, which are very Californian.

Rémoulade:

½ cup mayonnaise
2 teaspoons Creole or other grainy mustard
2 teaspoons Louisiana-style hot sauce
1 teaspoon lemon juice (reserve the rest of the lemon's juice and rind for the artichokes)
1 teaspoon prepared horseradish
1 teaspoon chopped capers
1 teaspoon smoked paprika
1 teaspoon chopped parsley
1 teaspoon pickle juice

Vegetable oil for frying
4 large artichokes
Juice and rind of 1 lemon (reserve 1 teaspoon for the rémoulade)
¾ cup flour
3 teaspoons Creole seasoning
2 eggs
1 cup bread crumbs
Salt and freshly ground pepper
4 hero rolls
2 cups shredded lettuce, such as romaine, Little Gem, or iceberg
2 tomatoes, sliced
15 pickle slices

To make the rémoulade:
Mix together the mayonnaise, mustard, hot sauce, lemon juice, horseradish, capers, paprika, parsley, and pickle juice until well combined. Season with salt and pepper.

To make the artichokes:
Heat 2 inches of vegetable oil in a deep pan to 350°F. Meanwhile, fill a bowl with water and add the lemon juice and the rind. Using a serrated knife, cut off the top one-third of the artichoke. Cut off 1 inch of the stem. Snap off the outer leaves until you can clearly see the yellow-green outline of the "heart." Cut off the remaining top part. Using a paring knife, carefully cut away any remaining green from the sides of the artichoke and the stem. Using a grapefruit spoon or a melon baller, remove the furry, fibrous "choke" at the center. Trim away any other green parts. Slice the heart into ½-inch-thick pieces and add them to the lemon water.

Place the flour in a shallow bowl. Add 1 teaspoon of the Creole seasoning and mix well. Crack the eggs into another shallow bowl and beat well. Place the bread crumbs in a third bowl, add the remaining 2 teaspoons Creole seasoning, and mix well. Place a wire rack over a sheet pan and set aside.

Remove the artichokes from the lemon water and pat dry with a paper towel. In two batches, dredge them in the flour, shaking off excess flour. Roll the artichokes in the egg and then in the bread crumbs, making sure they are well coated. Add the artichokes to the oil and fry until deep golden brown, 4 to 6 minutes. Transfer to the rack and immediately season with salt and pepper.

Spread each hero roll with a generous amount of rémoulade. Top with the lettuce, tomatoes, pickle slices, and fried artichokes.

Mac McDonald *of* Vision Cellars *in Sonoma*

The process of becoming accomplished in a career is never easy. It's even more challenging when you've chosen a profession that your family can't even dream of.

But Mac McDonald's journey from a small Texas town to being an acclaimed California winemaker and industry leader resembles a hero's journey. It started when he was twelve.

To say McDonald hails from a small town is an understatement. He grew up in Butler, a community about ninety miles south of Dallas that didn't even have a zip code. But he regularly met big-city folks because his grandfather took affluent men from Dallas and Fort Worth on hunting excursions. After a hunt one day, as visitors sipped moonshine made by McDonald's father, they started teasing a friend who had brought a bottle of French Pinot Noir on the hunting trip.

Until then, McDonald had seen only Thunderbird and the Muscadine, peach, or apple wine his family and neighbors made. "They were giving him a hard time about drinking Burgundy," McDonald recalls. "He looked at me and said, 'Would you like this bottle of wine?'" Mac's grandmother helped him cut into the cork, and he used a stick to push it into the bottle.

"I drank half of that bottle," he laughs, before his uncle took it away. "I said, this is really good. I want to be a winemaker." That idea stayed with him, and he told everyone about his dream to make wine. His high school basketball coach told him he needed to move to California. So, when he was invited to go visit Oakland in 1961, he jumped at the chance and ended up staying.

Odd handyman jobs turned into a career with the regional utility company, and McDonald did everything from buying and selling power off the grid to overseeing repairs to prevent fires. He kept searching for an entrée to wine country and eventually made his way up to Mendocino County, where the conditions are ideal for Pinot Noir.

He found a flavor profile for the fruit he liked. "We want that fruit to coat the inside of your mouth and pick up a little bit of sweet oak and cherries or berries or whatever that year gives us," he says. "We also want it to be able to go across the board with food."

He and his wife Lil launched Vision Cellars in 1995. Chuck Wagner of Caymus Vineyards fame let him use their winery facility, and McDonald still makes his wine at Joe Wagner's Copper Cane.

McDonald said he wanted to master Pinot Noir because it's the most challenging red grape. He's proud to be one of California's pioneering Black winemakers. But he makes it clear that he's a winemaker who just happens to be Black. "I don't call my wine Black wine. There ain't no such thing as Black wine. I make wine for everybody who's got dollars with white peoples' pictures on them. When you start trying to make wine for one side of the house, you're in trouble. Big trouble.

"I wanted to make wine to rival whatever the best of the best is," McDonald says. "I still feel that way today."

Smoked Trout Spring Salad *with* Lemon-Mint Vinaigrette

Yield: 4 servings   **Prep time:** 40 minutes
Cook time: 15 to 20 minutes

Fava beans are a labor of love in that they take some work to peel, but they're worth it—especially since their growing season is limited and their sweet, green flavor can be experienced for only a short time. Prep the favas a day ahead to make this dish super-fast.

Ice water for chilling
Salt
1 pound fava beans
1 bunch asparagus, trimmed
  and cut into 2-inch pieces
1 pound fingerling potatoes
4 scallions, white and green
  parts, thinly sliced
⅓ cup Marcona almonds
4 smoked trout fillets

Lemon-Mint Vinaigrette:
Juice and zest of 2 lemons
1 to 2 teaspoons granulated
  sugar
¼ cup fresh mint leaves,
  cut into chiffonade
¼ cup extra-virgin olive oil
Salt and freshly ground
  pepper

Bring a large pot of water to a boil. Fill a bowl with ice water and set it next to the stove. Add 1 tablespoon of salt to the boiling water. Remove the outer pods from the favas to expose the beans inside. Add the beans to the boiling water and cook for 1 minute. Remove the beans with a slotted spoon and place them immediately in the ice water. Once the beans have cooled, remove the outer whitish waxy skin of each bean by hand to reveal the bright green fava inside. Discard the skins and set the beans aside in a large bowl. Add fresh ice to the ice bath.

Add the asparagus to the boiling water and cook just until the pieces turn bright green but are still crisp, about 30 seconds. With a slotted spoon, transfer the asparagus to the ice bath. When the asparagus pieces have cooled, drain and add them to the beans.

Add the whole potatoes to the boiling water and cook until tender, about 15 minutes. Remove with a slotted spoon and set aside to cool slightly. When the potatoes are cool enough to handle, slice them into thick circles and add to the fava and asparagus. Add the scallions and almonds.

To make the vinaigrette:
In a blender, combine the lemon juice and zest, sugar, mint, and olive oil. Blend until smooth. Season with salt and pepper. Pour three-quarters of the vinaigrette over the fava mixture and toss to combine. Season with salt and pepper.

Gently flake the smoked trout. Spoon the fava mixture onto four plates. Top with the smoked trout and drizzle with the remaining vinaigrette.

Berbere-Spiced Braised Lamb Shanks *with* Spring Peas *and* Carrots

Yield: 4 servings   **Prep time:** 30 minutes, plus 45 minutes to 12 hours of marinating
Cook time: 3 hours

Berbere is a fragrant, traditional Ethiopian and Eritrean spice mix (there's a Moroccan version too) that brings spicy, bold, sweet, and aromatic flavor to anything it touches. Lamb shanks are a natural cut for this dish, yielding falling-off-the-bone meat tinged with the unctuousness of bone marrow.

Berbere Spice:

6 cardamom pods
3 chile de árbol pods, stems removed (see Note)
1 teaspoon fenugreek seeds
1 teaspoon coriander seeds
2 allspice berries
2 whole cloves
2 tablespoons paprika
1 tablespoon turmeric
1 tablespoon salt
¼ to ½ teaspoon cayenne pepper
½ teaspoon ground cinnamon
½ teaspoon ground ginger
¼ teaspoon ground nutmeg

4 lamb shanks, about 1 pound each
1 cup dry red wine
4 garlic cloves, thinly sliced
One 1-inch piece fresh ginger, peeled and thinly sliced
3 tablespoons neutral oil, such as grapeseed

To make the berbere spice:

Remove the pods from the cardamom to reveal the seeds inside and discard the pods. Combine the cardamom, árbol chiles, fenugreek, coriander, allspice, and cloves, and toast them in a small pan over low heat until fragrant, 3 to 5 minutes. Remove from the heat and allow to cool. Place the mixture in a spice grinder and grind to a fine powder. Place the mixture in a small bowl along with the paprika, turmeric, salt, cayenne pepper, cinnamon, ginger, and nutmeg and mix well. Store the spice mix in a sealed jar for up to 6 months.

Trim the lamb shanks of any excess fat. Rub 1 tablespoon of the spice mix onto each shank, covering generously. In a bowl, combine the red wine, garlic, and ginger, and pour the mixture over the lamb. Cover and let sit for at least 45 minutes at room temperature or refrigerate up to overnight.

Preheat the oven to 325°F.

Heat the oil in a large ovenproof pot or Dutch oven over medium-high heat. Remove the lamb from the marinade, scraping any garlic and ginger back into the marinade and reserving it. When the oil is hot, add the lamb and brown on all sides, about 4 minutes per side, 15 to 20 minutes total. Transfer the lamb to a plate and add the onions to the pot. Cook just until the onions start to brown,

continued

2 yellow onions, sliced

5 plum tomatoes, coarsely chopped

1 cup beef broth

Salt and freshly ground black pepper

16 spring carrots (with green tops for garnishing if available), peeled

1 cup fresh peas

Chopped fresh cilantro, for garnish

about 5 minutes. Add the tomatoes and cook until they start to break down, about 4 more minutes. Add the reserved marinade, the broth, and the lamb. Bring to a simmer, cover, and place the pot in the oven.

Cook until the lamb is very tender and starts to fall off the bone, 2 to 2½ hours. Remove the pot from the oven, transfer the lamb to a plate, and cover to keep warm. Blend the liquid and solids from the pot using a regular or immersion blender. Return the sauce to the pot, bring to a simmer, and reduce by 25 percent, about 5 minutes. Season with salt and pepper.

Add the carrots and simmer just until they are tender, 10 to 15 minutes. Nestle the lamb back into the pot. Turn off the heat, add the peas, and cover for 5 minutes. Place the lamb in a shallow bowl and spoon the sauce, carrots, and peas over the lamb. Sprinkle with cilantro and carrot greens.

Note: If you want the dish to be less spicy, remove the seeds from the chile de árbol pods before toasting and blending.

Mini Hoecakes *with* Crème Fraîche *and Caviar*

Yield: 40 little hoecakes or 12 to 14 large ones   **Prep time:** 15 minutes
Cook time: 10 minutes

These little cornmeal pancakes are a Southern classic with a California twist. The lore is that they once were made on the blade of a garden hoe over an open fire. They're heavier than crepes but still fluffy. Hoecakes are versatile with both salty and sweet toppings; try them as appetizers with salty smoked salmon or as full-size pancakes with syrup.

1¼ cups medium-grind
   cornmeal
¾ cup flour
1 teaspoon baking powder
1 teaspoon baking soda
½ teaspoon fine sea salt
1½ cups buttermilk
1 egg
4 tablespoons butter, melted,
   plus more for cooking
Caviar, ideally from
   California, for garnish
¼ cup crème fraîche
Chives for garnishing

Preheat the oven to 200°F.

In a large bowl, whisk together the cornmeal, flour, baking powder, baking soda, and salt. In a separate bowl, whisk together the buttermilk and egg. Add the wet ingredients to the dry ingredients and stir just until combined. Add the 4 tablespoons of the melted butter and stir to combine. Transfer the batter to a piping bag or a resealable plastic bag with the end snipped off.

Heat a large nonstick pan or griddle over medium-high heat. Melt 1 tablespoon butter in the pan. Pipe about 1 tablespoon of the batter into the pan per hoecake; do not crowd the pan. Cook until the hoecakes are browned on one side, about 2 minutes. Flip and cook until browned on the other side, 1 to 2 minutes more. Wipe out the pan in between batches and add fresh butter. Keep the hoecakes warm in the oven.

Top each hoecake with a dollop of caviar and crème fraîche. Cut the chives into 1½-inch batons and lay them on top of the hoecakes for garnish.

Rice-Flour–Fried Chicken Paillards *with* Arugula *and* Pea Shoot Salad

Yield: 4 servings
Prep time: 20 minutes, plus 15 to 30 minutes of marinating
Cook time: 15 minutes

You'll love this gluten-free, slightly lighter version of my signature buttermilk fried chicken from my restaurant Brown Sugar Kitchen. Since it uses only boneless breast meat, it doesn't need to marinate as long, and it's more tender and juicy than fried bone-in breasts. Adding a little of the buttermilk to the rice flour before dredging helps to give it the crunchy, craggy crust that you want in fried chicken.

4 boneless, skinless chicken breasts
1 cup buttermilk
2 tablespoons Creole seasoning
1 tablespoon pepper jelly (hot or sweet depending on preference)
2 tablespoons apple cider vinegar
¼ cup neutral oil, such as grapeseed
4 cups baby arugula
2 cups pea shoots
Vegetable oil for frying
1½ cups gluten-free rice flour
Salt and freshly ground pepper
Pickled Okra (page 44)

Place the chicken breasts on a sheet of plastic wrap and cover with an additional sheet. Using the flat side of a meat mallet, gently pound the breasts to an even ½-inch thickness. Be careful not to tear the meat.

In a large bowl, combine the buttermilk and 1 tablespoon of the Creole seasoning. Place the chicken in the buttermilk mixture and let marinate for 15 to 30 minutes.

In another bowl, whisk together the jelly and the vinegar. While whisking, drizzle in the neutral oil. Season with salt and pepper.

Place the arugula and pea shoots in a large salad bowl and set aside.

Heat 1 inch of vegetable oil in a large sauté pan over medium-high heat. Place a wire rack over a sheet pan near the stove.

Place the rice flour in a shallow dish and season with the remaining 1 tablespoon Creole seasoning. Drizzle 1 tablespoon of the buttermilk mixture into the rice flour and mix well to create little "bits." Lift the chicken pieces out of the buttermilk and dredge in the rice flour. In two batches, lay the chicken in the hot oil and fry until golden brown on both sides, about 3 minutes per side. Transfer to the wire rack and immediately season with salt and pepper.

Toss the arugula mixture with the pepper jelly vinaigrette. Lay one fried chicken paillard on each of the four plates and top with the salad.

Honey-Kumquat–Glazed Fresh Ham

Yield: 10 to 12 servings (1½ cups glaze)   **Prep time:** 10 minutes
Cook time: 4 hours 40 minutes

Kumquats, which grow wild in California, are striking with their dark green foliage studded with bright orange fruit. Try slathering this glaze on a cured, spiral-cut ham if you don't have the time to roast one.

One 8- to 10-pound fresh, bone-in ham
10 garlic cloves
2½ cups chicken broth
1 tablespoon salt
2 teaspoons ground coriander
2 teaspoons cumin
1 teaspoon freshly ground pepper

Honey-Kumquat Glaze:
8 ounces fresh whole kumquats
¼ cup honey
1 cup water
Salt and freshly ground pepper

Preheat the oven to 350°F.

Place the ham in a roasting pan, fat-side up. Score the fat on the ham diagonally about 1 inch apart, being careful not to cut all the way through the fat. Score the ham in the opposite direction to make a diamond pattern.

In a blender, combine the garlic, ½ cup of the chicken broth, salt, coriander, cumin, and pepper and blend to a paste. Rub the paste all over the ham. Pour the remaining 2 cups chicken broth into the pan. Cover tightly with aluminum foil and roast for 3 hours.

To make the glaze:

Rinse out the blender. Halve the kumquats and remove any seeds. Combine the kumquats and honey in a saucepan. Add the water and bring to a simmer. Let simmer until the kumquats start to turn translucent and soften, about 30 minutes. Remove from the heat and transfer to the blender. Carefully blend the mixture until smooth. Season with salt and pepper.

Remove the ham from the oven and uncover. Return the ham to the oven for 30 minutes, until the fat starts to crisp up. Remove the ham from the oven again and brush it all over with the glaze, making sure to coat it well. Return the ham to the oven and cook for 30 minutes. Remove the ham from the oven again, baste it with the pan juices, and cook for another 30 minutes. Check to make sure that liquid still remains in the bottom of the pan; if necessary, add an additional cup of broth or water. Continue this process until the internal temperature of the ham at its thickest part registers 165°F. Remove the ham from the oven and place it on a large platter. Place the roasting pan on the burner over medium-high heat and cook the juices down to a glaze, 6 to 8 minutes.

Serve the ham with the reduced glaze.

Grilled Monterey Bay Squid *with* Spicy Mustard-Green Salsa Verde

Yield: 4 main course servings, 8 appetizer servings
Prep time: 40 minutes, plus 20 minutes to 1 hour of marinating
Cook time: 5 minutes

While it's often battered and fried, I prefer grilling fresh California squid from Monterey Bay. The tender meat takes on a whole new dimension drizzled with this spicy green sauce flavored with mint, parsley, and serrano chile. Make sure your grill is very hot, so the squid cooks quickly and get a little charred.

Spicy Mustard-Green Salsa Verde:

½ shallot, chopped (about 2 tablespoons)
3 garlic cloves, chopped
1 serrano chile, stemmed and seeded
2 tablespoons capers
½ teaspoon red pepper flakes
¼ cup red wine vinegar
1 bunch mustard greens, (about 4 cups loosely packed)
¼ cup packed fresh mint
¼ cup packed fresh parsley
2 tablespoons packed fresh oregano
¾ cup extra-virgin olive oil
Salt and freshly ground black pepper

1 pound whole squid (preferably Monterey Bay), cleaned by the fishmonger

To make the salsa verde:

In a food processor, combine the shallot, garlic, serrano chile, capers, red pepper flakes, and vinegar, and pulse to combine. Add the mustard greens, mint, parsley, and oregano and pulse to chop coarsely. Add the olive oil and pulse a few more times. Season with salt and pepper.

To prepare the squid, separate the tentacles from the bodies. Slit the bodies up the side to open them up flat. Using a very sharp knife, make shallow slits diagonally across the bodies, being careful not to cut all the way through. Turn and make cuts in the opposite direction to make a crosshatch pattern. This will prevent the squid from curling up when cooking. In a large bowl, toss the bodies and tentacles with ½ cup of the salsa verde and marinate for at least 20 minutes or up to 1 hour. Thread the tentacles onto a skewer if they are very small. Alternately, after marinating, thread two skewers through the bodies so they will lie flat on the grill without curling.

Heat a grill to high heat. When the grill is very, very hot, lightly brush the grates with a little olive oil. Place the squid bodies and tentacles on the hottest part of the grill and cook just until they turn opaque and are lightly charred, about 1 minute per side. Be careful not to cook for too long or the squid will be chewy. Remove from the grill, sprinkle with salt, and serve with the remaining salsa verde.

Spring Slaw

Yield: 8 to 10 servings   **Prep time:** 45 minutes
Cook time: 0 minutes

The various textures and flavors in this non-cabbage slaw work together beautifully, and using crème fraîche instead of mayonnaise-based dressing keeps this tasting springy and light. This go-to side for any barbecue cuts the heaviness of meats and provides that bright flavor needed to balance out the meal.

1 small or ½ large jicama (about 10 ounces)
3 red radishes
1 watermelon radish
3 carrots, shredded (about 1½ cups)
1¼ cups thinly sliced sugar snap peas
4 scallions, white and green parts, sliced
¼ cup parsley
1 tablespoon chopped fresh tarragon
Salt and freshly ground pepper
½ cup crème fraîche
1 tablespoon champagne vinegar
1 tablespoon Dijon mustard
1 tablespoon honey

Cut off the top and bottom of the jicama to create two flat surfaces. Rest the jicama on one of the flat surfaces and remove its skin by using a knife to follow the curve of the jicama. Fit a mandoline with a julienne blade and carefully julienne the jicama, halving it if necessary to fit the mandoline. Alternately, finely shred the jicama using the largest holes on a box grater or the shredder attachment of your food processor.

Using the regular blade of the mandoline, slice the red radishes very thinly. Slice the watermelon radish thinly and then cut each slice into four pie-shaped pieces. Alternately, slice thinly with a knife.

Combine the jicama, both radishes, carrots, peas, scallions, parsley, and tarragon in a large bowl. Season with salt and pepper.

In a small bowl, whisk together the crème fraîche, vinegar, mustard, and honey and season with salt and pepper. Pour half of the dressing over the jicama mixture and toss well. Taste and add more dressing if desired.

Famous Black Restaurants

In 1947, Texas native and entrepreneur Lovie Yancey saved up her money, and with creativity and determination, she opened Mr. Fatburger, one of the first fast-food restaurants in the country. Yancey and her partner Charles Simpson scavenged scrap metal to build a three-stool hamburger stand on Western Avenue, near Jefferson Boulevard, in South Los Angeles's Exposition Park.

When Yancey and Simpson parted company, she dropped the "Mr." and continued under the name of Fatburger. She was determined to have the best quality burgers and insisted on using fresh ingredients to make her fries, sauces, milkshakes, and burgers in-house. Thanks to her professionalism and tasty food, Fatburger grew around Los Angeles. In 1973, she opened in Beverly Hills, and her fame was established. Celebrities such as Redd Foxx and Ray Charles named it their favorite burger place. By 1985, she started selling franchises, and within a year *Entrepreneur* magazine named Fatburger the "fifth fastest growing burger franchise." Yancey eventually sold the business, which now has more than 150 locations around the world.

On the other side of Los Angeles, in the Jefferson Park neighborhood, New Orleans cuisine found a home at Harold & Belle's. Harold Legaux Sr. and his wife Mary Belle opened their restaurant in 1969, serving Southern favorites: gumbo, po' boy sandwiches, red beans and rice, and shrimp Creole. This popular restaurant offered a place to eat, play pool, and celebrate Southern foodways and African American culture in Los Angeles. Harold and Belle's has been owned by the same family for three generations and remains an enduring culinary landmark.

But perhaps the most famous soul food restaurant in California is Roscoe's House of Chicken N' Waffles. It's been name-checked or featured in the movies *Jackie Brown*, *Swingers*, and *Rush Hour*. A native of Harlem, New York, Herb Hudson opened Roscoe's in 1975, and in the decades since, it's been adored by both the *New York Times* and former president Barack Obama. The combination of fried chicken and waffles wasn't typically served in the American South, although who's to say that they didn't share a table? Waffles were popular among some plantation elites, but they were not commonplace. The combo likely came from the Well's Supper Club in Harlem, where they were served in the 1930s to celebrities such as Sammy Davis Jr. and Nat King Cole. Roscoe's popularization of this dish—wherever its origins lie—cemented it to contemporary ideas of Southern cuisine and the West Coast.

Buttermilk Muffins *with* Cinnamon-Cardamom Streusel

Yield: 12 muffins   **Prep time:** 15 minutes
Cook time: 20 minutes

Just know that buttermilk makes almost everything more flavorful and moist. I also use butter instead of oil to amplify the flavor of the buttermilk, and this cardamom-cinnamon streusel makes these muffins stand out from others. You'll be amazed how quick it is to whip up a batch of these simple, no-mixer-needed muffins in the morning.

Cinnamon-Cardamom Streusel:

½ cup all-purpose flour
⅓ cup firmly packed brown sugar
2 teaspoons ground cinnamon
½ teaspoon ground cardamom
6 tablespoons unsalted butter, melted

2¼ cups all-purpose flour
⅔ cup granulated sugar
1 teaspoon baking soda
2 teaspoons baking powder
1 teaspoon fine sea salt
1 cup buttermilk
2 eggs
1 tablespoon vanilla extract
8 tablespoons unsalted butter, melted

Preheat the oven to 400°F. Line a twelve-well muffin tin with cupcake liners or spray with nonstick cooking spray.

To make the streusel:
In a bowl, stir together the flour, brown sugar, cinnamon, and cardamom. Mix in the butter and stir to make a thick, chunky paste.

To make the muffins:
Whisk together the flour, sugar, baking soda, baking powder, and salt. In a separate bowl, whisk together the buttermilk, eggs, vanilla, and melted butter.

Add the wet ingredients to the dry ingredients and stir just until combined. Using an ice cream scoop, evenly divide the batter among the muffin cups. Dab about 1 tablespoon of streusel over the top of each scoop of muffin batter—and don't be afraid to load it up, as the top will expand as the muffins bake.

Place the muffin tin in the oven and immediately turn the oven down to 350°F. Bake until golden brown and a toothpick inserted in the center comes out clean, 15 to 20 minutes.

Coconut Granola *with* Dried Tropical Fruits

Yield: Just over 8 cups granola, about 16 servings   **Prep time:** 15 minutes
Cook time: 35 minutes

For many people, California is granola country. It's associated with a vegetarian or healthy diet. I think it's always a good idea to have a go-to healthy snack to balance out all of the alternative temptations. I love packing this granola when I head out for a hike on the beautiful trails around Northern California. It's a palette for creating and combining the flavors and textures you love in a crunchy, slightly addictive package. In this Caribbean-inspired version, toasted coconut is delicious, and the buttery cashews melt in your mouth. You can use brown sugar if you can't find coconut sugar. But cardamom is essential; it adds a warm flavor and fragrance that makes this mix really stand out.

2 tablespoons water
¾ cup firmly packed dark coconut or brown sugar
¼ teaspoon ground cardamom
¼ teaspoon ground cloves
1 teaspoon salt
½ cup California Arbequina olive oil
4 cups rolled oats
1 cup dried coconut flakes (the larger kind)
1 cup roasted, salted cashews
2 tablespoons flaxseeds
2 tablespoons chia seeds
¼ cup chopped candied ginger
¾ cup chopped dried pineapple
¾ cup chopped dried mango

Preheat the oven to 300°F. Line a sheet pan or a baking sheet with parchment paper or a silicone mat.

In a small saucepan, combine the water and coconut sugar and heat over low heat just until the sugar is smooth and melted, about 2 minutes. Remove from the heat, add the cardamom, cloves, salt, and olive oil, and stir to combine.

In a large bowl, combine the oats, coconut flakes, cashews, flaxseeds, and chia seeds. Pour the warm olive oil mixture over the oat mixture and stir until everything is well combined and evenly coated.

Spread the granola in an even layer on the prepared sheet pan. Bake, stirring every 10 minutes, until the mixture is evenly browned, about 30 minutes total. Let cool completely in the sheet pan. Mix in the ginger, pineapple, and mango, and toss to combine well. The granola will keep in a jar for up to 4 weeks.

Freedom School Teaching
Farm *in Fresno*

Growing up in Fresno, the Reverend Floyd Harris remembers walking to school in the dirt, playing football in the street, and burning household trash and burying it in the backyard. That's because in the Black part of town, there were no parks, paved roads, or trash service. His grandma Bertha Harris and her church lady friends used to protest for civil rights and the same services as other neighborhoods.

Grandma Bertha and her husband Ike left Dumas, Arkansas, for Fresno in the 1950s looking for a better life. Even in California, they kept to their old ways, eating fresh vegetables from their garden and raising chickens. Floyd learned how to fry up a homegrown chicken, bake tea cakes, and use his voice to improve living conditions for his community.

"She was preparing me to be the man I am today," he says. "I didn't know Grandma was planting a seed." That idea grew into Freedom School & Farm, a program that teaches local kids how to grow food and how to grow into healthy and aware adults.

On a spring Saturday at the Free African Methodist Episcopal Church, the young farmers in the Freedom School farms harvest massive heads of romaine lettuce, pile them up for donations from shoppers, and serve salad and snow cones.

This is just one of four Freedom School farming sites in the area, including a plot in the front yard at Harris's home. Doing small-scale farming means they're getting in there with rototillers, rakes, and hoes to work the earth. That's fine with Taylon Gore. "I love lettuce. I love how we prepare the ground and take out the weeds. I've been here almost all my life," the twelve-year-old says. "I love digging in the dirt."

When he hatched the idea for Freedom School, Harris wanted to transform the way children like Taylon experience food. They live in the middle of the fertile Fresno Valley, yet their part of the city is a food desert. Harris says the 93706 zip code in Fresno has high concentrations of poverty, similar to areas of New Orleans that were devastated by Hurricane Katrina.

Aline Reed, the board president of the Freedom School, came out of retirement to help Harris realize his vision. Besides farming, the students learn life skills about nutrition, cooking, sewing, and photography, as well as how to clean a house, fix a car, and go out to dine with perfect table manners.

"We want to promote cultural wholeness for African American students," Reed says. "The kids learn to work together. If someone is acting up, the other student says, 'We don't do that at Freedom School.'"

They grow Fresno chiles and purple peas, but much of the produce, like okra, black-eyed peas, and yams, are foods from the African diaspora. They're learning to avoid fried and sugary foods, and that the meals they make at home are better-tasting and healthier than the processed food they buy.

"People right now with health and weight problems—their investment is in DoorDash instead of going into the kitchen and saying 'Let me make myself some black-eyed peas or a salad,'" Harris says. "My children today in our school understand what healthy food really is."

SUMMER

Watermelon, Jicama, *and* Little Gems Salad *with* Pecan-Parsley Vinaigrette *and* Shaved Parmesan

Yield: 6 to 8 servings   **Prep time:** 25 minutes
Cook time: 0 minutes

Watermelons originated in southern Africa and came to the Americas via the slave trade. Grown all over the southern United States, they made their way into soul food in all different ways: We eat slices plain, or with salt and pepper, and we even pickle the rinds. This salad pairs watermelon with jicama and lettuce and tosses it in a parsley dressing for a refreshing side with any summer meal.

Pecan-Parsley Vinaigrette:
½ cup chopped toasted pecans
1 cup packed fresh parsley
10 fresh mint leaves
2 garlic cloves
Juice of 1 lemon
1 teaspoon anchovy paste
¼ cup grated Parmesan cheese
½ cup extra-virgin olive oil
Salt and freshly ground pepper

2 heads Little Gem or 1 head butter lettuce
Salt and freshly ground pepper
2 cups cubed watermelon
½ cup julienned jicama (see page 66)
Zest of 1 lemon
Parmesan cheese for garnishing

To make the vinaigrette:
Combine the pecans, parsley, mint, garlic, lemon juice, anchovy paste, and Parmesan cheese in a food processor. Pulse until the mixture is finely chopped but still a little chunky. Add the olive oil and pulse until well combined. Season with salt and pepper.

Place the lettuce on a platter and season with salt and pepper. Scatter the watermelon, jicama, and lemon zest evenly over the lettuce. Drizzle with the vinaigrette and toss. Shave the Parmesan cheese over the salad.

African Crops and Harvest Traditions in America

Most people don't realize that many of the foods we eat in America come directly from Africa. Okra, black-eyed peas, rice, peanuts, yams, sweet potatoes, and watermelon are some of the crops that were brought from West Africa to the Americas during the transatlantic slave trade.

Watermelon originated from southern Africa and made its way across the continent to Egypt by 4000 BCE, where it is prominently featured in tomb paintings. This sweet melon was eventually brought to Asia, Europe, and across the Atlantic by 1576, where it is referenced as growing in Florida. It thrives in hot, dry fields and is an American favorite.

Sweet potatoes came from Central and South America, but the Portuguese brought them across the Atlantic and introduced them to West Africa where the yam (a similar tuber) was commonplace. Sweet potatoes made a handy substitute for African yams, and they were grown in Virginia as early as 1648, becoming an important part of early African American cuisine.

Peanuts, also known as groundnuts or goobers, came from South and Central America. They were brought to West Africa by Spanish colonizers, where they became a popular crop, and from there they made their way to America during the slave trade. In Virginia, these protein-rich nuts were ground to make dishes like peanut soup, a popular West African dish. In fact, many Virginians problematically consider peanut soup one of their native dishes.

Rice also came from Africa to the colonies, particularly the rice-growing areas of Georgia and Sea Islands in South Carolina. The Mende people from Sierra Leone were well-known rice cultivators and instrumental in the crop's success in the Low Country. American dishes like jambalaya are direct descendants of jollof rice, a traditional West African rice dish.

Black-eyed peas are another African ingredient that hold special standing in African American cuisine. Traditionally, they're eaten with greens on New Year's Day to bring good luck and money in the coming year. They're often used in the popular dish called hoppin' John, cooked with rice, onions, smoked meat, and seasoning; it is sometimes called Carolina peas and rice.

Okra is another important African vegetable that came across the Atlantic on the same ships that carried captured and enslaved African men, women, and children. Originally grown in Ethiopia, its seedy green pods were traded throughout Africa and the Middle East. This vegetable is eaten fried, pickled, curried, and in gumbo and stews throughout the African diaspora.

As these crops made their way across the country to the fields of California, they gave African Americans familiar foods as they adjusted to West Coast living. Today, rice is one of the top twenty most profitable crops in the state, which dominates the nation's agricultural markets.

Enslaved Africans and African Americans also brought a wealth of farming skills and culinary knowledge to fields and kitchens throughout the colonies. Their distinct cooking techniques of frying, one-pot meals, and barbecuing became synonymous with the newly developing American cuisine.

The fall harvest season provided a time to gather and take part in traditions once practiced in Africa and transferred to America. Harvest celebrations are important occasions throughout West Africa. The Igbo of Nigeria hold a well-known festival every August called *Emume iwa Ji na iri Ji ọhụrụ*, and it celebrates the yam harvest through dancing, music, and masquerade. These traditions survived and eventually were distilled into a distinctly African American harvest celebration. In 1966, in Los Angeles during the height of the Black Power movement, Ron "Maulana" Karenga invented Kwanzaa as an African American holiday, honoring elements of pan-African harvest festivals. The word *Kwanzaa* comes from the Swahili phrase *matunda ya kwanza,* meaning "first fruits of harvest," and it's observed from December 26 to January 1. It encompasses seven principles of African culture and community, including collective work and creativity. Symbols include corn (which signifies children), a chalice to inspire unity, and various fruits and vegetables that honor the labor of those who grew them.

While corn isn't native to Africa, its inclusion indicates the centrality of the crop to the history of African descendants in America. These harvest traditions celebrate African heritage and continue important traditions from the ancestors.

Charred Okra *with* Lime, Flaky Sea Salt, *and* Roasted Peanut Oil

Yield: 6 servings   **Prep time:** 10 minutes
Cook time: 8 minutes

Okra and peanuts came from West Africa to the Americas, and frying was an ancient cooking technique also transferred from African cultures to the American colonies. While overcooking brings out the natural slipperiness that gives okra an undeserved bad rap, even the most avid okra haters will adore this dish. The pods take on a lovely crunch and a hint of bitterness when you char them, while the sweetness of the honey-roasted peanuts and the lime's acid are a delicious match.

12 ounces fresh okra, rinsed well
2 tablespoons roasted peanut oil
Kosher salt and freshly ground pepper
Juice of 1 lime
¼ cup chopped honey-roasted peanuts
Flaky sea salt, such as Maldon

Preheat a grill to high heat.

Cut each okra pod into four pieces lengthwise. Gently toss with 1 tablespoon of the peanut oil and sprinkle with salt and pepper. Place the okra in a grill basket. Grill over high heat until browned and charred in some places, tossing as it cooks, about 8 minutes total. Remove from the heat and toss with the lime juice, peanuts, and the remaining 1 tablespoon peanut oil. Season with sea salt. Serve immediately.

Mixed Cucumber Salad *with* Fresh Herbs *and* Vinegar-Sugar Brine

Yield: 6 servings   **Prep time:** 15 minutes, plus 2 to 12 hours of marinating
Cook time: 0 minutes

When I was growing up, we had vinegary sliced cucumbers on the dinner table almost every night as a tangy condiment for rich fried chicken or salty ham hocked studded collard greens. This salad pays homage to my early food memories as a piquant side dish that compliments richer meats like barbecued ribs or pulled pork. Brined cucumbers give it a burst of sweet and sour, followed by a medley of fresh herbs and onions. It's also the perfect sidekick to a vegetarian spread.

½ cup white vinegar
2 tablespoons granulated
   sugar
2 teaspoons salt
2 English cucumbers, peeled
   and sliced ¼-inch thick
½ cup thinly sliced sweet
   onion (like Vidalia)
½ Fresno chile, seeded and
   thinly sliced (optional)
2 tablespoons chopped
   fresh dill
1 tablespoon chopped
   fresh mint
2 teaspoons chopped
   fresh thyme
Freshly ground pepper

In a small bowl, whisk together the vinegar, sugar, and salt until the sugar and salt are fully dissolved.

In a large bowl, combine the cucumbers, onion, chile, dill, mint, and thyme. Add the vinegar-sugar brine and toss to combine. Season with pepper. Refrigerate for at least 2 hours or up to overnight, stirring occasionally. Drain off the excess liquid and serve.

Black Food Entrepreneurs from Abby Fisher to Wally Amos

California has been home to several famous Black culinary legends. Two of them in particular, Abby Fisher and Wallace "Wally" Amos Jr., used their ingenuity and entrepreneurial spirit to turn their recipes into capital.

In 1880, Abby Fisher entered her pickles, sauces, and an assortment of jellies and preserved fruits into the fifteenth annual San Francisco Mechanics' Institute Fair. The judges, impressed with her entries, awarded her a bronze medal for best pickles and sauces and a silver medal for her jellies and preserves. One juror was later quoted as saying, "Her pickles and sauces have a piquancy and flavor seldom equaled, and, when once tasted, not soon forgotten." Mrs. Fisher knew how to cook, and everyone knew it.

Abby was born enslaved in 1831 on a South Carolina plantation to Abbie Clifton and a white father, a Frenchman named Andrew James. Abby eventually left South Carolina and lived in Mobile, Alabama, where she met and married Alexander C. Fisher, who would also become her business partner. They traveled west via Missouri before settling in San Francisco by 1880. Some historians think she may have signed on as a cook for the wagon train, helping finance her family's move to California.

It's clear that Abby's talents as a cook and savvy as a businesswoman shone once the Fishers arrived in San Francisco. She opened and ran the Mrs. Abby Fisher & Co.

pickle and preserves company and a catering business. Her pickled peaches, onions, watermelon rinds, and quince pear preserves were so beloved that her clients invested in her talents. Although Abby couldn't read or write, patrons helped her publish *What Mrs. Fisher Knows about Old Southern Cooking* in 1881, which was only the second cookbook authored by a Black woman in America. It brought Southern foodways and dishes like chicken gumbo and creole soup to San Francisco and the rest of the country. Having learned the art of cooking from her years as a plantation cook, she used those skills in California, where she influenced local cuisines and financially supported her eleven children and her husband, who worked as a porter.

She was not the only culinary superstar to find fame in California. Almost a century later in 1975, Wallace "Wally" Amos Jr. made his way to gastronomic fame with his cookies. Born in Florida in 1936, Amos attended high school at the Food Trades Vocational High School in New York. While he was living with his aunt, Della Bryant, she shared her cookie recipe with him, which he eventually turned into his own Famous Amos cookie recipe.

He joined the US Air Force and earned his GED before moving back to New York, where he secured an entry-level mailroom job at the William Morris Agency and moved up to become their first African American talent agent. Amos represented industry greats such as Diana Ross and Marvin Gaye, and he would use his cookies to lure potential talent.

When he was ready to launch Famous Amos Cookies in 1975, singers Marvin Gaye and Helen Reddy invested in his vision. By 1982, the cookies and his Famous Amos shops were bringing in more than twelve million dollars in revenue! In 1986, President Ronald Reagan gave Amos the Award of Entrepreneurial Excellence.

Brentwood Corn *and* Bellwether Ricotta Hushpuppies

Yield: Makes about 24 hushpuppies   **Prep time:** 15 minutes
Cook time: 55 minutes

Hushpuppies are a crowd favorite, although the origin of their name is debated. One version claims that leftover cornmeal batter was fried and then tossed to a nagging dog with the admonition, "Hush, puppy!" These particular puppies are made with light ricotta and Brentwood corn, a variety grown in the Sacramento River Delta that is renowned for its sweetness and perfection. I love these puppies as an appetizer, a side dish, or even as an in-between-meal nibble.

2 cobs fresh sweet corn, preferably the Brentwood variety, shucked

¾ cup medium- or coarse-grind cornmeal

½ cup all-purpose flour

2 tablespoons granulated sugar

½ teaspoon baking soda

½ teaspoon salt

½ teaspoon freshly ground pepper

2 eggs

⅓ cup buttermilk

⅓ cup fresh ricotta, preferably from Bellwether Farms

¼ cup grated yellow onion (about ½ small onion)

3 cups vegetable oil for frying

Toasted Pecan Romesco (page 153) or Rémoulade (page 48) for serving

Fill a saucepan with about 1 inch of water, then set a steamer on top. Bring the water to a gentle boil over medium-high heat. Snap the corncobs in half and place in the steamer. Cover and steam until crisp-tender, about 30 minutes. Transfer the cobs to a cutting board. When they're cool enough to handle, stand up each cob half on its end and cut away the kernels as close to the cob as possible. You should have about 1 cup of corn kernels.

In a bowl, whisk together the cornmeal, flour, sugar, baking soda, salt, and pepper until well combined. In another bowl, whisk together the eggs, buttermilk, and ricotta until well combined. Make a well in the flour mixture and add the wet ingredients. Use a fork to gently stir the mixture together just until moistened. Add the corn kernels and onion and stir until combined.

Add the oil to a deep 12-inch cast-iron skillet. Line a large rimmed baking sheet with paper towels. Over high heat, warm the oil to 375°F on a deep-fry thermometer. Using two spoons, drop tablespoonfuls of the batter into the oil. Do not overcrowd the pan; you will need to do this in batches. Cook, turning the hushpuppies once or twice with a heatproof slotted spoon or tongs, until they're richly browned and cooked through, about 6 minutes. Transfer to the prepared baking sheet. Repeat to cook all the batter.

Serve right away with romesco or rémoulade.

Ashlee Johnson-Geisse *of* Brown Girl Farms *in Hayward*

Ashlee Johnson-Geisse, founder of Brown Girls Farms, has had farming in her DNA for generations. Her father's family farmed peanuts in Virginia for decades, and her mother's Texas family grew fruit and vegetables on a two-acre parcel when they moved to Los Angeles.

Today, Ashlee and her wife, Jennifer Johnson-Geisse, run a farm and community-supported agriculture (CSA) service that feeds nearly forty families in the East Bay. Ashlee feels honored that her seventy-eight-year-old grandmother, Hedy Felix, helps them pack produce boxes each week. "We're an intergenerational farm, which you don't find all the time," she says. "It's part of our legacy as Black people."

When the pandemic began, Ashlee had just left her role as a senior garden educator at a Berkeley middle school. Even though she and Jen were isolated in their Berkeley apartment, Ashlee wanted to teach and help people discover the joys of growing food. Soon, the women were tending plants in a small greenhouse on the roof of their building.

She started sharing photos of their rooftop garden with friends and through Instagram. "The pandemic really opened up people's eyes to see that they can grow things, especially with the pressure on our food systems," Ashlee says. "I was like, I'm gonna answer that call. As soon as I opened the business, the community found us through social media."

Ashlee's dad imagined radio spots saying: "Come on down to Brown Girl Farms where we put soul in your bowl," Johnson-Geisse says with a laugh. And the name stuck.

Soon they were driving around the East Bay, making contactless deliveries of mixed mustard greens, purple snap peas, strawflowers, herb bundles, and vegetable seedlings. They included cards with inspirational quotes and seed packets hand-painted by Ashlee. "It was like a mini-CSA," Jen says.

It was a warm-up for the CSA they would run on their homestead tucked away in the hills above Hayward and Castro Valley. A small inheritance from a relative who loved gardening allowed them to purchase the property and transform it into a farm.

With the help of friends and farming fellows, Ashlee and Jen hand-dug thirty beds using Native American and ancestral farming know-how. Deep furrows help water soak into the ground better, and coplanting purple basil alongside tomatoes helps both plants thrive. Now the farm teems with life, from the beds of bachelor's buttons and sunflowers to the coop with squawking chickens to the humming beehives. The fifteen mature apple trees already on the property add a sweet touch to their produce boxes.

Besides giving people clean food to eat, Ashlee says that they, as queer-identifying farmers, want to welcome more people of color and LGBTQIA+ folks to farming. "It's a welcoming space for you to be who you are," she says. "Whatever pronouns you use and however you identify, you're going to be respected here."

Cornmeal Dough Pizzette *with* Grilled Beefsteak Tomatoes, Red Onions, *and* Whipped Goat Cheese

Yield: 2 small pizzettes, 4 to 6 servings   **Prep time:** 25 minutes, plus 1 hour rise time
Active time: 45 minutes

The tomato season is long here in California, and grilling beefsteak tomatoes caramelizes their natural sugars and adds a nice texture to the slices. The cornmeal adds more chew and a little sweetness. You'll love this heartier mini-pizza as an appetizer or a main course. Pour yourself a big glass of local rosé or Chardonnay and put this sweet thing on the grill!

Pizzette Dough:
1 cup warm water
One ¼-ounce packet yeast
1 teaspoon granulated sugar
2 cups flour, plus more for dusting
¾ cup cornmeal, plus more for dusting
1 teaspoon fine sea salt
1 tablespoon extra-virgin olive oil

Whipped Goat Cheese:
8 ounces goat cheese
2 tablespoons fresh oregano, plus more for garnishing
1 teaspoon red pepper flakes, plus more for garnishing
1 garlic clove
2 tablespoons honey
¼ cup extra-virgin olive oil
Kosher salt and freshly ground pepper

To make the dough:
Combine the warm (110°F) water with the yeast and sugar and let it sit until foamy, or about 5 minutes. In a small bowl, whisk together the flour, cornmeal, and sea salt. Add the yeast mixture to a stand mixer fitted with a dough hook. Add the olive oil. Add the flour mixture and mix on low speed until combined and the dough has turned into a ball that climbs up the dough hook, about 5 minutes. Turn the dough out onto a lightly floured surface and form it into a smooth ball. Place it in a lightly oiled bowl, cover with a towel, and put the bowl in a warm place until the dough has doubled in size, about 1 hour.

Preheat the grill to high heat.

To make the cheese:
In a food processor, combine the goat cheese, oregano, red pepper flakes, garlic, honey, and olive oil and process until smooth. Season with salt and pepper.

Slice the tomatoes into ½-inch-thick slices and place on paper towels to absorb some of the moisture. Sprinkle with salt and let sit for 3 minutes. Pat the slices with paper towels. Drizzle the tomatoes

continued

2 large beefsteak tomatoes

1 small red onion, thinly sliced

Extra-virgin olive oil for drizzling

with olive oil, coating both sides. Place the tomatoes on the grill and cook just until they show grill marks but aren't soft, about 30 seconds per side. Remove and set aside.

Once the dough has risen, punch it down and turn it out onto a lightly floured surface. Divide the dough into two pieces. Pat and stretch each piece into a round or oblong shape. Dust a pizza peel or the back of a sheet pan with cornmeal. Place one pizzette on the peel. Turn one side of the grill to low heat. Slide the pizzette onto the low-heat side of the grill and close the cover. Grill just until the dough starts to set and the bottom is lightly marked, about 1 minute. Flip the pizzette and grill the other side just until marked, about 1 minute more. Remove the pizzette from the grill and return to the peel. Repeat with the remaining dough.

Spread one pizzette with half of the whipped goat cheese. Top with an even layer of the grilled tomatoes. Top with half of the thinly sliced onion. Return to the low-heat side of the grill, cover, and grill until the cheese is melted and the dough is fully cooked, turning as needed to prevent charring, 5 to 8 minutes total. Repeat with the other pizzette and the remaining cheese, tomatoes, and onion.

Remove from the grill and sprinkle both pizzettes with oregano, red pepper flakes, and olive oil.

Barbecued Pulled Tofu Sandwich

Yield: 4 servings   **Prep time:** 12 minutes
Cook time: 35 minutes

As more and more of us African Americans turn to plant-based diets, the range of dishes available has expanded into soul food. I created this barbecued tofu sandwich as a way for vegetarians, vegans, or anyone who likes to mix it up to enjoy all the rich flavors and textures of a barbecue sandwich, but without the pork! Add a little slaw, and you'd think you were in Tennessee. A single varietal chile and not a chile powder blend will provide a richer unique flavor.

Barbecue Sauce:
¼ cup vegetable oil
1 yellow onion, diced
6 garlic cloves, minced
2 cups canned plum
  tomatoes with juice
2 tablespoons red wine
  vinegar
1 tablespoon Dijon mustard
1 tablespoon honey
1 tablespoon ground
  California chile
  (not chili powder)
1 teaspoon toasted cumin
  seed, ground in a mortar
  or spice grinder
1 teaspoon salt
¼ teaspoon cayenne pepper
¼ teaspoon freshly ground
  black pepper

Two 5-ounce packages Hodo
  Soy tofu skin strips (yuba)
4 whole-grain hamburger
  buns, toasted
Mango chow-chow or
  bread-and-butter pickles
  (optional)

To make the barbecue sauce:

In a large saucepan, heat the oil over medium heat. Add the onion and garlic and sauté until the onion softens slightly, about 5 minutes. Transfer the onion and garlic to a blender or food processor along with the plum tomatoes, vinegar, mustard, honey, California chile, cumin, salt, cayenne pepper, and black pepper. Puree until smooth, and then return the sauce to the pan (no need to clean it out first). Bring to a simmer over medium-low heat and cook for 10 to 15 minutes to blend the flavors.

While the sauce cooks, slice the tofu skins into ⅓-inch-wide strips. Then gently pull the stacked skins apart into fettuccine-like strands. Add the tofu skins to the sauce and let simmer just until they're coated with sauce and hot throughout.

Lightly toast the buns in a toaster oven, in a hot oven, or under a broiler. Place the bottom half of each bun on a serving plate. Top with the tofu skin strips, dividing them evenly. Cover with the top bun. Serve immediately with mango chow-chow or pickles on the side, if desired.

Baked Eggs in Stewed Cherry Tomatoes *with* Chopped Fresh Herbs *and* Buttery Cornbread Crumbs

Yield: 4 to 6 servings   **Prep time:** 10 minutes
Cook time: 40 minutes

This is a play on shakshuka, a North African dish made from seasoned stewed tomatoes and eggs. We use fresh tomatoes of different hues in this version, which bring color and tartness to the dish, while cornbread crumbs add California soul food flair. This is a perfect brunch dish, and it's best served from stove to table, family-style, in the skillet it was cooked in.

1 cup crumbled cornbread

1 teaspoon chopped fresh thyme, plus 2 sprigs

1 teaspoon chopped fresh rosemary, plus 1 sprig

1 pinch cayenne pepper

2 tablespoons unsalted butter, melted

Salt and freshly ground black pepper

3 tablespoons extra-virgin olive oil, plus more for drizzling

3 garlic cloves, thinly sliced

1 small shallot, thinly sliced

2 pints mixed cherry tomatoes

6 eggs

10 fresh basil leaves

Preheat the oven to 375°F.

In a bowl, combine the cornbread, 1 teaspoon of the thyme, 1 teaspoon of the rosemary, cayenne pepper, and butter and toss well. Sprinkle with salt and black pepper. Line a sheet pan with a silicone mat or parchment paper, and evenly spread the mixture on top. Bake until golden brown, about 8 minutes. Remove from the oven and allow to cool. The mixture will continue to crisp up as it cools.

Heat a 10-inch cast-iron skillet over medium-high heat. Add the olive oil, garlic, and shallot and sauté just until the garlic and shallot soften a little but don't brown, about 2 minutes. Add the cherry tomatoes, thyme sprig, and rosemary sprig, and sauté, stirring, until the cherry tomatoes start to soften and burst, 7 to 10 minutes. Season with salt. Gently and carefully mash the tomatoes down with a spoon. Remove the herb sprigs and discard.

Make six wells in the tomato mixture and crack the eggs into them. Gently move the tomatoes so the egg whites sink to the bottom of the skillet. Turn the heat down to a gentle simmer and cook until the whites begin to set, 2 to 3 minutes. Season with salt and pepper and transfer the skillet to the oven. Bake just until the whites are set but the yolks are still runny, about 6 minutes. Remove from the oven and sprinkle with the cornbread crumbs. Tear the basil over the mixture, drizzle with a little more olive oil, and serve immediately.

Dirty Potato Salad *with* All the Peppers *and* Onions

Yield: 6 servings   **Prep time:** 20 minutes
Cook time: 25 minutes

This potato salad gets its name from all its seasonings, which make the potatoes look a little dirty. But I think dirty is a good thing when you're talking martinis or the signature rice in New Orleans. Every bite is bold and fresh, thanks to the rainbow of peppers and sweet onions.

2 pounds new potatoes, quartered
1 lemon, halved
Salt and freshly ground black pepper
1 tablespoon Creole seasoning, plus 2 teaspoons
2 tablespoons neutral oil, such as grapeseed
1 red bell pepper, stemmed, seeded, and chopped
1 green bell pepper, stemmed, seeded, and chopped
1 yellow bell pepper, stemmed, seeded, and chopped
1 Vidalia or other sweet onion, chopped
1 garlic clove, minced
¾ cup mayonnaise
1 tablespoon grainy mustard
2 tablespoons Worcestershire sauce
1 teaspoon chopped fresh thyme
1 teaspoon soy sauce
3 scallions, white and green parts, thinly sliced
1 tablespoon chopped fresh chives

Place the potatoes in a large saucepan and cover with cold water by 1 inch. Squeeze in all the juice of the lemon and then toss in the lemon halves. Season with 2 teaspoons salt and 1 tablespoon of the Creole seasoning. Bring to a boil over medium-high heat and cook just until the potatoes turn tender, about 15 minutes. Drain the potatoes and discard the lemon.

Heat the oil in a large sauté pan over medium-high heat. Add the red, green, and yellow bell peppers and onion and sauté until they soften and just start to brown, 8 to 10 minutes. Add the garlic and cook for 1 minute. Season with salt and black pepper. Remove from the heat.

Toss the potatoes with the bell pepper and onion mixture.

In a separate bowl, whisk together the mayonnaise, mustard, Worcestershire sauce, the remaining 2 teaspoons of the Creole seasoning, thyme, and soy sauce. Season with salt and black pepper. Pour this dressing over the warm potatoes, bell peppers, and onion and toss well to coat. Sprinkle with the scallions and chives and serve.

Barbecued Oysters *with* Bacon-Vinegar Mignonette

Yield: 6 servings   **Prep time:** 10 minutes
Cook time: 10 minutes

I never had barbecued oysters until I moved to California, but I'm a convert. Oysters grow all along the California coast, and they're so flavorful cooked right in their shells. The star of this recipe is the sauce, which is basically a cross between a mignonette, a barbecue sauce, and the classic butter of a broiled oyster. Because the grill does the hard work of opening the shells, this dish comes together very fast and you don't need to have ever shucked an oyster before. It's even easier with pre-shucked oysters—just skip the initial minute on the grill.

Bacon-Vinegar Barbecue Mignonette:

3 slices bacon, chopped
1 small shallot, minced
1 garlic clove, chopped
1 tablespoon tomato paste
2 tablespoons champagne
   vinegar
1 teaspoon smoked paprika
1 teaspoon brown sugar
Kosher salt and freshly
   ground pepper
3 tablespoons unsalted
   or slightly salted butter,
   softened

3 cups coarse salt (like
   kosher salt)
2 dozen oysters, scrubbed
Chives for garnishing

To make the mignonette:

Cook the bacon over medium-high heat in a sauté pan until well browned and crispy, about 5 minutes. Transfer the bacon to a paper towel with a slotted spoon. Add the shallot and garlic to the bacon fat in the pan and cook just until softened, about 2 minutes. Add the tomato paste, stir well, and cook for 1 minute. Add the vinegar and scrape the bottom of the pan. Add the paprika and sugar and mix well. Season with salt and pepper. Remove from the heat and let cool.

Add the cooled mixture and the reserved bacon to the softened butter and stir to combine well. This mignonette can be made up to 1 day in advance and stored in the fridge.

Preheat a grill to high heat. Line a platter with the coarse salt.

Place the oysters on the grill, deeper shell-side down. Close the lid and cook just until the oysters open a tiny bit, about 1 minute. Remove them from the grill and pry them fully open with an oyster knife, carefully removing the top shell and slicing through the area where the oyster is attached to the shell. Keep as much "liquor" (the liquid inside the shell) as possible in the oyster.

continued

Barbecued Oysters, *continued*

Place a heaping ½ teaspoon of the mignonette inside each oyster. Place the oysters on the grill, close the lid, and cook just until the butter melts and the oysters bubble a little, 1 to 2 minutes. Place the oysters on the salt-lined platter and garnish with chives. Serve immediately.

Grilled Shrimp *and* Corn *with* Avocado White Barbecue Sauce

Yield: 4 main course servings, 6 appetizer servings   **Prep time:** 15 minutes
Cook time: 15 minutes

White barbecue sauce is popular in Alabama and a few other spots in the Deep South. It's very different from the tomato- or vinegar-based sauces of the Upper South or the dark red Texas-style sauce. Normally white barbecue sauce is pale, thanks to its mayonnaise. But this one delivers the creaminess of that classic sauce with the richness and beautiful green color of California avocados. You'll marvel at the way this pale sauce elevates fresh corn and grilled shrimp.

Avocado White Barbecue Sauce:

1 ripe avocado
1 garlic clove
1 tablespoon grated yellow onion
¼ cup mayonnaise
2 tablespoons white vinegar
1 tablespoon prepared horseradish
1 tablespoon Worcestershire sauce
1 tablespoon grainy mustard
Juice of 1 lemon
1 teaspoon hot sauce
1 teaspoon granulated sugar
Salt and freshly ground pepper

1 pound extra large (16 total) shrimp, peeled and deveined, tails left on
3 ears of corn, shucked
2 tablespoons neutral oil, such as grapeseed

Soak four wooden skewers in water for at least 30 minutes.

To make the barbecue sauce:
In a food processor, combine the avocado, garlic, onion, mayonnaise, vinegar, horseradish, Worcestershire, mustard, lemon, hot sauce, and sugar and process until smooth. Season with salt and pepper. Reserve ¼ cup of the sauce to brush onto the shrimp and set aside the remaining sauce.

Preheat a grill to medium-high heat.

Thread four shrimp onto each skewer. Brush the corn with the oil and sprinkle with salt and pepper. Place the corn on the hottest part of the grill and cook, turning, until the corn is tender, cooked through, and a little charred in places, about 8 minutes total. Remove the corn from the grill to cool.

Brush the shrimp skewers with the reserved ¼ cup sauce and season with salt and pepper. Place the skewers on the hottest part of the grill and cook until the shrimp turns opaque and pink, 1 to 2 minutes per side.

Slice the kernels off the corncobs and place on a platter. Top with the shrimp skewers. Drizzle generously with sauce, and serve any remaining sauce on the side.

Miss Oddette's Barbecue Sauce
from Paso Robles

Oddette Augustus was just two years old when her great grand-daddy Edward Tip Scott passed on. But she grew up hearing family stories about how he had left Lake Charles, Louisiana, in the 1910s to start a scandalous new life in California. "My great-grandfather was a pimp," she says. "He pimped his way from Louisiana to California and settled in Stockton on the port."

The Gold Rush helped trans-form Stockton, a sunny coastal town surrounded by fertile farm-land, into a booming commercial port and shipbuilding center. And with the deepest channel in the world, it welcomed cargo ships from Russia, Europe, and South America. And so did Tip Scott's bordello, which offered sailors far from home some company and diversions.

Her grandparents, Hazel and Ruben Smith, didn't want to raise their children in Jim Crow Louisiana, so they too moved to Stockton in the 1930s. With his family in town, Tip knew it was time to become more respectable. He closed his business, married his madam, and started growing vegetables. "He couldn't be the town pimp with grandchildren," Augustus laughs.

Hazel enjoyed Stockton's warmth, while Ruben liked fishing in the Delta's thousand miles of waterways. They loved their new life, but raising four kids during the Depression didn't leave much money for extras like eating at restaurants.

"They couldn't afford to go buy barbecue, so my grandfather made a pit out of a barrel, she made the sauce, and they satisfied their children," Augustus says. Grandma Hazel, who the kids called "Granga," made a big batch of spicy barbecue sauce every spring.

Even before she could reach the stove, Augustus was her grand-ma's kitchen helper. They made the sauce together in March or April and let it sit for a couple of months. "We wouldn't eat it until Memorial Day, and it would last all summer," she says. Everyone in the family got a few jars to use for their weekend barbecues.

Eventually, Augustus took over making sauce for her family. When she retired from her job with the state, she started a cater-ing business that sold barbecue, macaroni and cheese, potato salad, and white beans laced with barbe-cue sauce, ground turkey, onions, and green peppers that she calls *Muddy Beans*. But right from the start, her barbecue sauce was the star. She sold cases of it at a local farmers' market and won awards. For a time, her sauces were in almost every grocery store along the Central Coast.

"It's just a basic sauce," she says humbly. "It's my family recipe with garlic from Gilroy and onions from California." The sauce comes in two styles: the spicy No Joke that's her grandmother's original recipe, and Special Report, which is less potent. "You get this nice kick at the end. It's going to make you sweat but it's not going to hurt." Both sauces are available on her website.

Smothered Warm Grilled Tri-Tip *with* Spinach

Yield: 6 servings **Prep time:** 15 minutes, plus 4 to 12 hours of marinating
Cook time: 1 hour

When I moved to California, I discovered the tri-tip, a quintessential California cut made famous in the Santa Maria area. This recipe brings together the mustard, molasses, and brown sugar found in a typical barbecue sauce for a perfect beef marinade. The sugars caramelize on the grill, and you end up with a gorgeous hunk of juicy beef that's ready to slice and serve on a bed of spinach. The onions on top add an extra layer of flavor and texture to the meat. When you want to feast on beef and that grill is calling, try this stunner!

One 2- to 2½-pound
  tri-tip steak
Salt
1 cup dry red wine
6 garlic cloves
2 tablespoons coarsely
  ground pepper
1 tablespoon mustard seeds
1 tablespoon molasses
1 tablespoon liquid aminos
¼ cup neutral oil, such as
  grapeseed, plus more for
  oiling the grill
1 large red onion, thinly
  sliced
1 tablespoon brown sugar
4 cups loosely packed
  fresh spinach

Trim any silverskin (connective tissue) from the tri-tip steak. Sprinkle generously with salt. In a food processor, combine the red wine, garlic, pepper, mustard seeds, molasses, liquid aminos, and oil and process until well combined. Place the steak in a plastic bag and cover with the red wine mixture. Refrigerate for at least 4 hours or up to overnight, massaging the bag every couple of hours.

Preheat a grill to medium-high heat. Remove the steak from the marinade, reserving the marinade. Pat the steak dry with paper towels and set aside.

Place the red onion slices in a pile in the center of a 24-inch piece of heavy-duty aluminum foil and toss with the brown sugar, salt, and pepper. Pull up the edges of the foil all the way around, and pour 1 cup of the reserved marinade over the onions. Fold the foil over and seal to create a pouch. Place the foil pouch on the grill and cook, flipping every 5 minutes, until the onions are tender and caramelized, 20 to 25 minutes.

Meanwhile, oil the grill grates lightly with oil. Place the steak on the hottest part of the grill and cook until well marked and browned, about 2 minutes. Flip the steak and cook the other side until well browned, about 2 more minutes. Turn off half of the grill or move the coals to one side. Move the steak to the cooler part of the grill and cook to the desired doneness, turning occasionally, 25 to 30 more minutes for medium rare (125 to 130°F on an instant-read thermometer). Remove the steak from the grill and let it rest for 10 minutes.

Slice the steak thinly against the grain. Arrange the spinach leaves on a platter and the steak slices atop the spinach. Place the onions and any reserved juices over the steak and spinach.

Grilled Rack of California Lamb *with* Collard-Almond Pesto

Yield: 4 servings and about 1¾ cups pesto   **Prep time:** 20 minutes
Cook time: 21 minutes

Sonoma lamb is a flavorful delicacy, and it shines with lighter herbs like mint or parsley to balance the flavors. This collard-almond pesto is a delicious, hearty alternative to the traditional version. The collards, a soul-food staple, take on a new life as a raw, fresh pesto made with crushed almonds. One of my favorite combos is serving it with my Grilled Plums and Onions (page 123) or simply mashed sweet potatoes.

Collard-Almond Pesto:
½ bunch collard greens, center ribs removed and coarsely chopped, about 4 cups
4 garlic cloves
¼ cup grated Parmesan cheese
Juice and zest of 1 lemon
⅓ cup roasted almonds
½ cup extra-virgin olive oil, plus 1 tablespoon
2 tablespoons warm water
Salt and freshly ground pepper

One 6- to 8-bone California rack of lamb

Preheat a gas or charcoal grill for indirect grilling so that one side is hot. Brush the cooking grates clean.

To make the pesto:
Combine the collards, garlic, Parmesan cheese, lemon juice and zest, almonds, ½ cup of the olive oil, and warm water in a food processor. Process until well combined. Season with salt and pepper. Remove half of the pesto and set aside for serving.

Season the rack of lamb with salt and pepper. Drizzle with the remaining tablespoon of olive oil. Place the lamb, meat-side down, on the hot part of the grill. Grill until the meat is well marked, about 2 minutes. Flip and cook until the bone side is also well browned, about 4 more minutes. Move the meat to the cooler side of the grill, bone-side down. Brush with the reserved half of the pesto, close the lid, and cook to the desired temperature (10 to 15 more minutes for medium rare, depending on the size of the rack).

Antoine Ellis *and* Cedric Jefferson *of* Compton Farms USA *in Compton*

The city of Compton has a rough-and-tumble image, since it's the birthplace of seminal rappers such as Dr. Dre, Kendrick Lamar, and N.W.A. But few people know that this Los Angeles bedroom community has been rooted in agriculture since the late 1800s.

In 1887, founding father Griffith Compton donated the land to form the town on the condition that a vast section would be devoted to agriculture. Black families who had left the South flocked to the Richland Farms area, where they had room to have large gardens, cows, chickens, livestock, and stables for horses. Antoine Ellis was pretty much destined to be a cowboy. From an early age, he rode horses with one of the community equestrian groups in Compton.

And now he's got cattle to go with it. Ellis and childhood friend Cedric Jefferson are reviving Compton's pastoral history with Compton Farms, their homegrown brand offering beef, chicken, sausage, and eggs. Their goal is to make sure people in their community have fresh, healthy, high-quality food to eat. "I cannot wait to be able to provide the inner city with premium food at a reasonable, affordable rate," Ellis says.

On a Saturday in 2021, Ellis and Jefferson looked like city slickers in their matching deep red polo shirts, western jeans, and black cowboy boots. They were in Lemoore to check on their cows and a new calf. The cattle are all of the Angus breed, and they're getting them certified by the USDA.

"I guess healthful eating started it off for me," says Jefferson. "We're eating our way into diabetes," Ellis says. "Let's eat our way out of diabetes." They both liked the idea of being self-sufficient, like people were in previous generations, and helping their relatives and friends achieve the same independence from the commercial food system, which isn't equitable.

"The Ralphs in Beverly Hills and the inner city get different kinds of food," says Jefferson. "We get whatever is left over, and it's the bottom of the barrel. It's always grade B or C. It's second-class stuff. It's been sitting, and it's been picked over by nicer neighborhoods."

Demand is high already: Friends and family snapped up all 626 pounds of rib-eyes, T-bones. and burgers from their first steer in just two weeks. They have a website set up to sell their products, and they'll be working with a discount store in Compton to sell their beef.

Renting farmland rather than owning it keeps many Black farmers from achieving financial security, so Ellis and Jefferson were determined to buy their own ranch. Their day jobs (Ellis owns a trucking company and Jefferson is a senior engineer with the water department) enabled them to purchase a seven-acre parcel near Perris, California. Dwayne Allen, another urban cowboy, manages the barn and takes care of the growing herd.

Next, they're buying tractors so they can plant a field for the cattle to graze in so they can be certified as grass-fed beef. The acreage offers plenty of room for chickens that will go into their spicy Compton Farms chicken sausage, as well as birds for egg production. "Our chickens won't be put under a light and forced to lay eggs," Jefferson says. Planting vegetables and fruits like melons and berries is the next phase of the plan. They'll use integrated pest management, where helpful bugs eat harmful ones, and grow their crops without pesticides.

Ellis is also involved in Urban Saddles, a Compton community organization that teaches young people how to ride and care for horses.

Becoming a farmer reminds Ellis of his dad, Frank Ellis Sr. Frank was originally from Alligator, Mississippi, and left to join the military. He fought in the Korean War and during World War II, he was in the last regiment of the Buffalo Soldiers. "My dad always raised his own food: rabbits, chickens, and a garden," says Ellis. Now he's proud to be doing the same on a bigger scale.

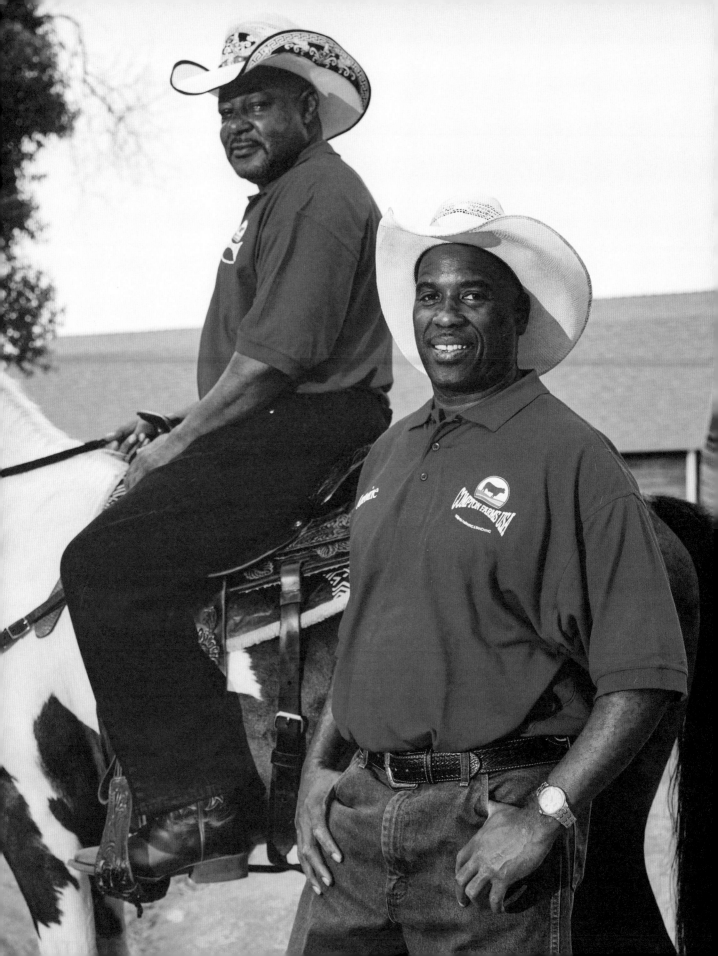

Juneteenth

For the first time in 2021, Juneteenth was celebrated as a federal holiday. It commemorates the day in 1865 that Major General Gordon Granger brought the news of freedom to the enslaved communities in the former Confederate stronghold of Galveston, Texas. Accompanied by US troops, Granger announced General Order No. 3, which stated in no uncertain terms that "all slaves are free."

This was nearly three years after President Abraham Lincoln issued the Emancipation Proclamation and less than two months after the end of the Civil War. Notifying the slave community that its members were free was the responsibility of their masters, who kept hundreds of thousands of African Americans enslaved beyond the end of the war.

On June 19, 1866, exactly one year after the news made it to Galveston, Juneteenth was born. The name is a mix of two words, *June* and *nineteenth*, and it has been commemorated for more than 150 years. Celebrated with parades, barbecues, dances, and the singing of spirituals, the holiday quickly became a yearly occasion to feast with family and loved ones.

Across the country, other emancipation days were similarly celebrated with cookouts and music. Some are called Jubilee Day or Freedom Day, but Juneteenth, while nationally significant, was more popular in Texas and the surrounding states. The holiday spread westward with the Great Migration, becoming part of California's culture.

Juneteenth also brings specific culinary traditions to the table. Texas-style barbecue traveled west and became central to Juneteenth celebrations. Known for dry rubs and smoked meats like beef brisket, this distinct style moved seamlessly into African American-owned restaurants in Los Angeles, Oakland, and Sacramento.

Most Juneteenth menus include barbecued meats, red beans and rice, collards, cornbread, watermelon, red drinks (strawberry, hibiscus, or lemonade), cobblers, and of course some red velvet cake. Red is significant as this color of dye was reserved for the wealthy during slavery. Using it in these foods represented the upward mobility of newly freed people and their ability to eat what they wanted. It's a holiday that celebrates not just the end of chattel slavery, but also the beautiful cuisines of Africans in America. Neighborhood cookouts, church gatherings, parades, music, dancing, and family barbecues are all part of these traditions.

Texas was the first state to formally recognize Juneteenth in 1980, and California adopted it in 2003. The holiday continues to bring people together through food. Over the past several decades, activists have advocated for Juneteenth to be a federal holiday. One woman in particular made sure it happened. In 2016, Ms. Opal Lee, then an eighty-nine-year-old activist, walked from her home in Fort Worth, Texas, to Washington, DC, to lobby for a federal Juneteenth holiday. Lee is known as "the grandmother of Juneteenth," and her efforts were recognized by President Joe Biden's administration during the signing of the declaration on June 17, 2021.

While the holiday has been observed in Black communities for decades, the 2020 Black Lives Matter protests brought Juneteenth into mainstream consciousness.

Grilled Plums *and* Onions

Yield: 4 servings   **Prep time:** 10 minutes
Cook time: 8 minutes

Plums in every color, from red and purple to green and gold, grow plentifully here in California. They're most often eaten fresh out of hand, sliced for salads, or slipped into desserts, but grilling them brings out a deeper flavor balanced by bright acidity. Pairing them with onions and tossing them in the grill transforms them into a sophisticated and tasty accompaniment for any meat.

½ large sweet onion (such as Vidalia), cut into ½-inch-thick rings
2 plums, halved and pitted
3 tablespoons extra-virgin olive oil
Salt and freshly ground pepper
2 tablespoons California Zinfandel or other very dry red wine
2 teaspoons red wine vinegar
2 teaspoons brown sugar
8 basil leaves, thinly sliced
4 cups loosely packed baby arugula

Preheat the grill to high.

In a bowl, carefully toss the onion rings and plums with 1 tablespoon of the olive oil and season with salt and pepper. Try not to break up the onion rings too much. Grill the onions and plums until they are well marked and the onions are soft, about 4 minutes per side. Remove from the grill and let cool enough to handle.

Thinly slice each plum half. In a bowl, whisk together the Zinfandel, vinegar, and sugar. Drizzle in the remaining 2 tablespoons olive oil while whisking. Season with salt and pepper and add the basil. Toss the arugula with the plums, onions, and vinaigrette.

Fig *and* Almond Crostatas

Yield: Eight 6-inch crostatas   **Prep time:** 20 minutes, plus 30 minutes to 12 hours of chilling time
Cook time: 25 minutes

I still remember eating my first fig in Louisiana off my grandparents' tree and tasting my grandmother's fig preserves and pies. These crostatas, or tartlets, are the perfect dessert to showcase the California fig in all its glory. The small amount of almond paste provides just enough nuttiness to balance with the rich fruit. Be sure to use figs that are at the peak of ripeness.

Dough:
2¼ cups all-purpose flour, plus more for dusting
1 cup unsalted butter, cut into cubes and chilled
2 tablespoons granulated sugar
1 teaspoon salt
4 to 7 tablespoons ice water

Filling:
7 ounces almond paste
3 tablespoons crème fraîche
¼ teaspoon salt
6 fresh Black Mission figs
1 egg, beaten
3 tablespoons Demerara sugar

To make the dough:
Combine the flour, butter, sugar, and salt in a food processor and pulse until the mixture resembles small peas. Add 4 tablespoons of the ice water and pulse just until the dough holds together when pressed between your fingers. If necessary, add more water, 1 tablespoon at a time. Be careful not to overprocess.

Turn the dough out onto a lightly floured surface and press lightly to form a disk. Wrap with plastic wrap and refrigerate for at least 30 minutes or up to overnight.

On a lightly floured surface, roll out the dough into a 16- to 17-inch circle, ¼ to ⅛ inch thick. Cut into eight 6-inch circles, rerolling the scraps if necessary to form more dough. Line a sheet pan with a silicone mat or parchment paper. Place the dough circles on the pan and put in the refrigerator to keep them chilled.

Preheat the oven to 375°F.

To make the filling:
Crumble the almond paste into a food processor. Add the crème fraîche and salt and process until smooth.

Cut each fig into four pieces lengthwise. Place about 1 tablespoon of the almond paste in the center of each circle. Top with three fig slices. Gently fold the edges of the dough over the edge of the almond paste and figs, pinching and sealing to make a border, but leaving the center exposed. Brush the crust with the beaten egg and sprinkle each tart with about 1 teaspoon of the coarse sugar. Bake until the crust is golden brown and the figs are caramelized and bubbly, 20 to 25 minutes. Serve warm or at room temperature.

Peach *and* Pecan Clafoutis

Yield: 6 to 8 servings   **Prep time:** 20 minutes
Cook time: 1 hour

A clafoutis (cluh-FOO-tee) is a cross between a cake and custard. It always features meltingly ripe fruit, so it resembles a cobbler in some ways. French and African foodways and recipes melded in places like Haiti and New Orleans, and the result was Creole cuisine, a particular style of soul food. This dish is one of those reminders of the versatility of classic, but simple recipes. Fragrant ripe peaches and butter form the flavor base, and pecans add a lovely crunch in this summer dessert. Dust it with confectioners' sugar, or pair it with whipped cream and enjoy it warm from the oven.

1½ pounds firm peaches
4 tablespoons unsalted butter
¼ teaspoon ground
  cinnamon
1 cup granulated sugar
¾ cup pecan pieces
4 eggs
1 cup whole milk
1 tablespoon apple or
  French brandy
1½ teaspoons vanilla extract
1 pinch of salt
½ cup all-purpose flour
Whipped cream or ice cream
  for serving

Heat the oven to 375°F.

Prepare the peaches by peeling, removing the pits, and slicing.

Heat a 10-inch cast-iron pan over medium heat and add the butter. Add the peaches, cinnamon, and ¼ cup of the sugar and cook until the peaches are softened, about 10 minutes.

Place the pecan pieces in a food processor and pulse until the mixture forms a small crumb, but not as fine as a flour.

In a medium-size bowl, whisk together the eggs, the remaining ¾ cup sugar, milk, brandy, and vanilla. Whisk in the pecans and salt, and then slowly whisk in the flour to avoid lumps.

Pour the pecans over the peaches and bake for 10 minutes at 375°F. Then lower the temperature to 350°F and cook for an additional 35 minutes, until golden.

Serve warm with whipped cream or ice cream.

Honey Lavender Chess Pie

Yield: 8 servings   **Prep time:** 30 minutes, plus 30 minutes to 12 hours of chilling time   **Cook time:** 1 hour

The origin story of chess pie is unclear. Some say it came from an enslaved cook who referred to her nutless, fruitless pie as "just pie" and it was misheard as "chess pie." Others say the name came from the pies being stored in a chest to keep cool. Either way, it's a custard-style pie that's common throughout the Deep and Upper South.

Dough:
2¼ cups all-purpose flour, plus more for dusting
1 cup unsalted butter, cut into cubes and chilled
1 teaspoon salt
4 to 7 tablespoons ice water

Filling:
½ cup heavy cream
1 tablespoon dried lavender buds
8 tablespoons (½ cup) butter, room temperature
1 cup honey
7 egg yolks
2 tablespoons medium- or coarse-grind cornmeal
Confectioners' sugar for garnishing

To make the dough:
Combine the flour, butter, and salt in a food processor and pulse until the mixture resembles small peas. Add 4 tablespoons of the ice water and pulse just until the dough holds together when pressed between your fingers. If necessary, add more water, 1 tablespoon at a time. Be careful not to overprocess. Turn the dough out onto a lightly floured surface and press lightly to form a disk. Wrap with plastic wrap and refrigerate for at least 30 minutes or up to overnight.

On a lightly floured surface, roll out the dough into a 15-inch circle. Transfer to a 9-inch pie dish and trim the edges. Crimp the edges and return the dough to the refrigerator to keep it chilled.

Preheat the oven to 350°F. Place parchment paper over the dough and fill with pie weights or dried beans. Bake just until dough starts to cook, about 8 minutes. Remove pie weights and cook just until the dough starts to look dry, about 5 minutes. Remove from the oven.

To make the filling:
Combine the cream and lavender in a small saucepan and bring to a simmer over medium-low heat. Remove from the heat and let cool. Once cool, strain out the lavender and discard.

Combine the butter and honey in the bowl of a mixer. Beat until the butter is light and fluffy and the honey is incorporated, scraping down the sides of the bowl as necessary, about 3 minutes. Add the egg yolks, lavender cream, and cornmeal and mix until incorporated. Pour the mixture into the prepared pie shell.

Bake until browned and the filling is almost set in the center, about 45 minutes. If the crust is getting too brown, tent the pie loosely with foil. Remove from the oven and let cool completely. Dust with confectioners' sugar before serving.

Blueberry, Cornmeal, *and* Candied Lemon Tea Cakes *with* Olive Oil

Yield: 12 cakes **Prep time:** 25 minutes, plus cooling time for the candied lemons
Cook time: 15 minutes

Teacakes hold special significance for families originally from the South. These recipes are treasured, and they're served only on special occasions. These sweet baby cakes are not only beautiful, but the blueberries and cornmeal give them a distinct texture while the California olive oil adds incomparable richness. You can use any lemon, but I adore the fragrance of candied Meyer lemon zest.

Candied Lemons:

2 lemons
1 cup granulated sugar
1 cup water

½ cup granulated sugar
¼ cup olive oil, preferably
  a California variety
1 egg
¾ cup all-purpose flour
¾ cup medium- or coarse-
  grind cornmeal
½ teaspoon baking powder
½ teaspoon baking soda
½ teaspoon fine sea salt
¼ cup buttermilk
½ cup blueberries

To make the candied lemons:

Zest one lemon and set the zest aside. Squeeze the juice of that lemon into a small saucepan. Thinly slice the other lemon into at least twelve slices. Add the sugar and water to the saucepan and bring to a simmer over medium heat. Once the sugar is dissolved, add the lemon slices and let simmer gently until they turn translucent, turning occasionally, about 15 minutes. Transfer from the liquid and place on a silicone mat or a wire rack until fully cooled.

To make the teacakes:

Preheat the oven to 350°F. Spray a twelve-well muffin tin with nonstick cooking spray.

In a large bowl, whisk together the sugar, olive oil, and egg. In a separate bowl, whisk together the flour, cornmeal, baking powder, baking soda, and salt. Add the dry ingredients, the reserved lemon zest, and the buttermilk to the egg mixture and stir just until combined and no lumps remain.

Place 1 heaping tablespoon of batter into each muffin well. Top with a few blueberries and press one lemon slice gently over the top of the berries. Bake for 15 minutes until golden brown and a toothpick inserted in the center comes out clean. Let the teacakes cool for 5 minutes, then gently turn them out onto a wire rack. Turn them back over with the lemon slices facing up and cool completely before serving.

Watermelon Pisco Cocktail

Yield: 1 cocktail

Pisco is a white grape brandy from Chile and Peru, and its clean flavor is sublime with refreshing, juicy watermelon. You can adjust this cocktail's sweetness by reducing the melon and increasing the pisco. Tajín is a branded spice blend of Latin chiles, dehydrated lime, and salt.

Tajín
Lime wedge for rimming
    the glass and garnishing
    (optional)
Ice
2 ounces pisco
½ ounce Aperol
1 ounce watermelon juice
½ ounce simple syrup
    (see page 183)
¾ ounce lime juice

Rim a Collins glass with lime and then dip the rim in Tajín, if desired. Fill the glass with ice and set aside.

Combine the pisco, Aperol, watermelon juice, simple syrup, and lime juice in a cocktail shaker, and shake well for 30 seconds. Strain into the prepared glass, garnish with the lime wedge, and serve.

Hibiscus Lemonade Spritzer

Yield: 6 to 8 servings (64 ounces)

Hibiscus originated in either India or Africa, where it's brewed into a tangy red drink known as *bissap*. In Mexico, it's mixed with warm spices in a beverage called *jamaica*, while it goes by the name *sorrel* in the Caribbean. This spritzer's bright red color and light taste make it the perfect addition to a seltzer water or cocktail; it uses sparkling water and a splash of lemonade. Make a huge pitcher because everyone will want seconds.

Hibiscus Syrup:

1 cup water
1 cup granulated sugar
1 cup dried hibiscus leaves

1 pint lemon juice
1 pint Hibiscus Syrup
  (see above)
2 pints sparkling water
Lemon wedges for
  garnishing

To make the syrup:

In a pan, bring to a boil the water, sugar, and hibiscus leaves. Once the sugar has dissolved, turn off the heat, let cool, and strain the syrup through a fine sieve.

In a large pitcher, whisk together the lemon juice, hibiscus syrup, and sparkling water. Chill and serve over ice, garnishing with a lemon wedge.

Blackberry Gin Shrub

Yield: Makes 4 to 6 cocktails (12 ounces of shrub)

Blackberries grow wild all along the California coast and throughout the southern United States too. Combined with sugar and vinegar, the berries make a delicious shrub, which is an acidic and sweet base for drinks. Shrubs have been used since Victorian times to preserve delicate, ripe fruits. They can be used in cocktails like this one or as a nonalcoholic drink with club soda or seltzer. This blackberry shrub mixed with gin, soda, and lime instantly creates a refreshing cocktail.

Blackberry Shrub:

2 cups (12 ounces) fresh
  or frozen blackberries
  or raspberries
⅔ cup apple cider vinegar
½ cup granulated sugar

2 to 3 ounces Blackberry
  Shrub, or to taste
  (recipe follows)
2 ounces gin
½ ounce fresh lime juice
3 ounces club soda
Blackberries, lime wedges,
  and fresh mint sprigs for
  garnishing (optional)

To make the shrub:

In a small saucepan over medium heat, stir together the blackberries, vinegar, and sugar. Bring to a simmer, then lower the heat to low and cook gently, stirring, until the blackberries have completely disintegrated, about 10 minutes. (Use a potato masher or a fork to help break down the blackberries.) Remove from the heat and set aside to cool completely. Strain the mixture through a fine-mesh strainer into a bowl, pressing it with a rubber spatula to extract all the juices. Transfer the liquid to a glass jar. Cover and refrigerate until chilled, at least 1 hour. The shrub can be stored in the refrigerator for up to 1 week.

For each cocktail, combine the chilled blackberry shrub, gin, and lime juice in a cocktail shaker filled with ice. Shake well for about 30 seconds, then strain into an ice-filled glass, filling it about three-quarters full. Top off with club soda. Garnish with a few blackberries, a wedge or twist of lime, and a sprig of mint if desired.

Coconut Rum Picnic Punch (Three Little Birds)

Yield: 1 shaken drink or 8 servings for blended version

Rum was perfected in Barbados during the 1600s, where it was first called *kill-devil* or *rumbullion*. Regardless of whether you like your rum white, spiced, or aged, it's one of the most popular spirits in the world. This rum punch gives a nod to the three spirits' Afro-Caribbean roots and is the ultimate picnic punch. Just be sure to serve it with lots of ice to make sure it stays nice and chilled. Cheers!

Shaken Version:
1 ounce white rum (Barbados or Jamaica)
½ ounce aged rum
½ ounce Herbsaint liqueur
1 ounce Coconut Cream Syrup (recipe follows)
2 ounces pineapple juice
½ ounce lime juice
Maraschino cherry for garnish
Pineapple wedge for garnish

Blended Version:
1 cup white rum (Barbados or Jamaica)
½ cup aged rum (Wright & Brown)
½ cup Herbsaint liqueur
1½ cups Coconut Cream Syrup (see below)
2½ cups pineapple juice
½ cup lime juice

Coconut Cream Syrup:
Two 400-ml cans coconut milk
2½ cups granulated sugar
2 pinches salt
1 tablespoon whole cloves
½ teaspoon ground nutmeg

To make the shaken version:
Fill a glass with ice cubes. Fill a cocktail shaker with ice and add the white rum, aged rum, Herbsaint liqueur, coconut cream syrup, pineapple juice, and lime juice. Shake well for 10 seconds, and double-strain into the prepared glass. Garnish with a maraschino cherry and a pineapple wedge.

To make the blended version:
In a blender, combine the white rum, aged rum, Herbsaint liqueur, coconut cream syrup, pineapple juice, and lime juice, and four cups of ice. Blend until smooth. Pour into chilled glasses and serve right away.

To make the coconut cream syrup:
In a saucepan, bring the coconut milk, sugar, salt, cloves, and nutmeg to a boil. Lower the heat and let simmer for 10 minutes, stirring frequently. Cool and strain. This mixture can be stored in the refrigerator for up to 1 month.

FALL

Roasted Beets *and* Fennel

Yield: 4 to 6 servings   **Prep time:** 15 minutes
Cook time: 25 minutes

Beets are abundant in so much of California's cuisine because they're easy to grow, packed with nutrients, and pretty delicious! Fennel, the delicious aromatic, anise-flavored vegetable, literally grows out of the cracks in the sidewalks here. Roasting the two creates a beautiful natural sweetness and depth of flavor. This dish is so savory and filling that you could easily eat this as a main course. Just keep the two separated during roasting to prevent the fennel from turning pink.

1 head fennel, cored and cut into ½-inch wedges, fronds reserved and chopped to yield ¼ cup

4 small beets (1½ pounds), peeled and cut into ½-inch wedges

2 tablespoons extra-virgin olive oil, plus more for drizzling

½ teaspoon ground fennel seeds

½ teaspoon ground cumin

Salt and freshly ground pepper

Juice and zest of 1 lemon

2 tablespoons chopped Italian parsley

Preheat the oven to 400°F.

Place the fennel on one half of a baking sheet in a single layer. Arrange the beets on the other half in one layer. Drizzle 2 tablespoons of the olive oil over the fennel and beets, sprinkle with fennel seeds and cumin, and season with salt and pepper. Toss, keeping the beets and fennel separate.

Roast until the beets are tender and the fennel is cooked and caramelized, about 25 minutes. Remove from the oven and sprinkle with lemon juice, lemon zest, and parsley. Scatter the reserved fennel fronds over the beets and fennel. Drizzle with olive oil. Serve hot or at room temperature.

San Francisco Bay Area

The San Francisco Bay Area was one of the big destinations for African Americans moving westward during the Gold Rush. The early Black settlers were met with limited jobs and mostly worked in the service industry as maids, porters, and cooks. In 1916, San Francisco's white restaurant workers unionized and went on strike, while African Americans, who were not allowed to join the union, temporarily worked as strikebreakers in the food industry.

The early twentieth century brought jazz and blues to the Bay Area, and "Harlem of the West" cities like Oakland and San Francisco quickly became hubs for Black-owned or operated businesses. The music of New Orleans traveled fast via the railroad, and jazz legends like Harold Padeo moved from Louisiana and settled in Oakland, where the Black music scene was in full swing by the 1920s. The Creole Café, Pantages Theatre, Musicians Music Club, and Sweet's Ballroom were some of the hot spots for music and food in early Oakland.

In West Oakland, Seventh Street was the spot for blues and barbecue. Slim Jenkins opened a liquor store in 1933 that later expanded to a nightclub and a popular supper club that hosted the likes of Aretha Franklin, Nat King Cole, B.B. King, the Ink Spots, and Dinah Washington. One of the waitresses at Slim Jenkins Supper Club, Esther Mabry, decided to open her own spot in the then-bustling Black business district in West Oakland. In 1950 she opened Esther's Breakfast Room, which later grew into Esther's Orbit Room, which offered cocktails and live music. San Francisco, home to Etta James and Sugar Pie DeSanto, had a booming supper club scene as well. These spaces provided places for Black culture to flourish and for soul food to continue to influence the broader culture.

Barbecue was synonymous with Oakland during the 1960s and 1970s. Seventh Street was lined with Black-owned restaurants: Earle's Famous Bar-B-Que, Burk's Seafood & Barbeque, Singer's Bar-B-Q, Crissie's Barbeque Pit, and Field's Bar None Bar-B-Q. Other locations were home to Flint's Bar-B-Q, established in 1968, and Everett & Jones, started in 1973.

Oakland was also home to dozens of family-owned soul food restaurants, like Dorsey's Locker and Holiday Fish Market, which are both closed, and Lois the Pie Queen, which has been serving up soulful breakfasts, fried chicken, and pies for more than sixty years. Brown Sugar Kitchen stood on the shoulders of these great institutions, and it continued the tradition of offering delicious soul food to Oaklanders and all who visited.

Shaved Brussels Sprouts Salad *with* Warm Bacon Dressing

Yield: 6 servings **Prep time:** 12 minutes
Cook time: 10 minutes

I know I've been preaching plant-based eating, but bacon makes nearly everything taste better. Smoked and cured meats, especially pork, have been key soul food seasonings for centuries. Today, I use only sustainably raised heritage pork. Once you taste the bacon from Black Pig Meats, you'll understand the difference. Typically, the meat would be cooked down with greens or beans. Here, shaved brussels sprouts make a beautiful side dish that is sure to hit the marks on both texture and flavor.

1½ pounds small brussels sprouts, ends trimmed and any blemished outer leaves removed

Warm Bacon Dressing:
6 slices applewood-smoked bacon, chopped
1 tablespoon grainy Dijon mustard
2 teaspoons honey
¼ cup apple cider vinegar
Salt and freshly ground pepper

Use a mandoline, a very sharp knife, or the thinnest slicing blade on a food processor to very thinly slice the brussels sprouts into fine shavings. Transfer to a serving bowl and, using your hands, fluff and separate the shavings.

To make the dressing:
In a pan over medium heat, fry the bacon until brown and crisp and the fat is rendered, about 5 minutes. Using a slotted spoon, transfer the bacon pieces to a paper towel to drain, then sprinkle over the brussels sprouts. Reserve ¼ cup of the bacon fat in the pan and discard the rest or save for another use. Rewarm the reserved fat over medium heat, then whisk in the mustard, honey, and vinegar until well combined.

Drizzle the dressing over the shaved brussels sprouts and season with salt and pepper. Toss gently and serve.

Sweet Potato Gnocchi *with* Spinach

Yield: 4 servings
Prep time: 25 minutes, plus potato cooking and cooling time   **Cook time:** 55 minutes

Let's talk about yams and sweet potatoes, two life-sustaining foods for flavor, nutrients, and culture. We love them cooked any way, but in this recipe, sweet potato shines differently, bathed in savory garlic butter, Parmesan cheese, and a splash of balsamic vinegar. The gnocchi dough is soft and requires a light touch.

2 large sweet potatoes
  (1 pound)
1 egg
1½ cups all-purpose flour,
  plus more for kneading
  and dusting
1 teaspoon baking powder
½ cup grated Parmesan
  cheese
Salt and freshly ground
  pepper
3 tablespoons unsalted butter
1 garlic clove, chopped
2 tablespoons balsamic
  vinegar
4 cups loosely packed
  spinach leaves

Preheat the oven to 375°F.

Place the sweet potatoes on a baking sheet and roast until a knife is easily inserted and the potatoes are tender, about 45 minutes. Remove from the oven and let cool.

Peel the skins off the potatoes, add their flesh to a large bowl, and mash until smooth. Add the egg and mix well. In a separate bowl, stir together the flour, baking powder, and ¼ cup of the Parmesan cheese until well combined, and season heavily with salt and pepper. Add the flour mixture to the sweet potato mixture. Gently mix until everything is combined. Turn out the dough onto a floured surface and gently knead until a smooth but soft ball is formed. The dough should be soft but not sticky. If dough is still too sticky, add more flour, 1 tablespoon at a time.

Dust a baking sheet generously with flour. Bring a large pot of salted water to a boil. Generously dust the work surface with flour. Divide the dough into four balls. Roll each ball into a rope that is ¾ inch in diameter. Cut the rope into 1-inch pieces and place them on the floured baking sheet. Make sure the gnocchi aren't touching so they don't stick to one another. Carefully add the gnocchi to the boiling water and gently stir. Boil until the gnocchi start to float, about 2 minutes. Reserve 1 cup of the pasta water and drain the gnocchi.

In a large skillet over medium-high heat, melt the butter. Add the garlic and cook for 1 minute, being careful not to brown it. Add the vinegar and cook for 1 minute, stirring. Add the gnocchi, ¼ cup of the pasta water, and the spinach to the pan and gently toss well until the spinach is wilted. Add additional pasta water as necessary to make a sauce. Sprinkle with the remaining ¼ cup Parmesan and toss well. Pour into a serving bowl.

Butternut *and* Acorn Squash, Pear, *and* Goat Cheese Gratin

Yield: 8 servings   **Prep time:** 25 minutes
Cook time: 50 minutes

When fall comes, local farmers markets fill up with winter squashes,
I reach for this recipe. A play on traditional potato gratin, this vivid
version blends two naturally buttery squashes with California red
pears and tangy goat cheese. You can peel the squash if you prefer,
but the baked skins are tender and look really pretty.

1 small butternut squash
  (2 pounds)
1 small acorn squash
  (1 pound)
2 California red pears
2 tablespoons fresh thyme
Salt and freshly ground
  pepper
1 cup heavy cream
1 shallot, thinly sliced
1 pinch ground nutmeg
Juice of 1 lemon
8 ounces goat cheese,
  crumbled

Preheat the oven to 375°F.

Spray a 9 by 13-inch baking pan with nonstick cooking spray.

Halve the butternut squash lengthwise and remove the seeds.
Slice the squash into ⅛-inch-thick slices. Halve the acorn squash
lengthwise and remove the seeds. Slice into ⅛-inch-thick slices.
Slice the pears into ⅛-inch-thick slices. Arrange the squash and
pear slices in alternating layers in the pan, so it's butternut, acorn,
and then pear. Repeat until all the ingredients are used. Sprinkle
with thyme and generously season with salt and pepper.

Combine the cream, shallot, nutmeg, lemon juice, and half
of the goat cheese in a small saucepan and bring to a simmer
over low heat. Stir until the goat cheese is fully melted. Pour the
mixture evenly over the squash and pears, making sure the shallot
is evenly distributed. Top with the remaining goat cheese. Cover
with aluminum foil and bake for 30 minutes. Uncover and bake
until the squash is tender and fully cooked and the top is golden
brown, about 15 minutes more.

Collard Green Tabbouleh

Yield: 6 to 8 servings **Prep time:** 25 minutes
Cook time: 10 minutes

Although tabbouleh is traditionally made with tons of fresh parsley, this version features collards. In Southern cuisine, collard greens are usually slow-cooked until tender. But used raw, these hearty leaves add a wonderful texture and vegetal complexity to the salad, not to mention a nutritional boost. Use a food processor to cut down on the chopping time. You'll love how the mint makes the whole thing pop!

1 cup water
½ cup bulgur wheat
1 bunch collard greens
1 cup packed fresh mint
3 plum tomatoes, seeds
 removed and diced small
3 scallions, chopped
Juice and zest of 1 lemon
¼ cup extra-virgin olive oil
Salt

Combine the water and bulgur in a small saucepan over medium-high heat. Bring to a boil, lower the heat to a simmer, and cook until the bulgur is tender and the water has evaporated, about 10 minutes. Remove from the heat, cover, and let sit for 10 minutes. Uncover and fluff with a fork. Set aside to cool.

Remove the center ribs from the collards and discard or save them for another use. Tear the leaves, add them to a food processor, and pulse until they are finely chopped but not pureed. Add the collards to a large bowl. Add the mint leaves to the food processor and pulse until coarsely chopped but not pureed. Add the mint to the collards. Add the cooled bulgur, tomatoes, scallions, lemon juice and zest, and olive oil and mix well. Season with salt. Let sit for at least 1 hour before serving.

Zucchini-Scallion Waffles *with* Toasted Pecan Romesco

Yield: 4 servings, 4 large waffles **Prep time:** 25 minutes
Cook time: 20 minutes

Waffles don't always have to be sweet; after all, my famous cornmeal waffles are very savory. These delicious zucchini-scallion waffles are a hit for both their texture and flavor, and their crispy edges and nooks provide the perfect surface for the silky romesco. Romesco, a Spanish sauce, is usually made with almonds, but here pecans add rich nut flavor that ties the whole dish together.

Toasted Pecan Romesco:
1 plum tomato, halved
   lengthwise
1 teaspoon extra-virgin olive
   oil, plus 2 tablespoons
One 7-ounce jar roasted
   red peppers, drained
   (or fresh piquillo peppers)
1 garlic clove
½ cup toasted pecan pieces
1 teaspoon smoked paprika
2 tablespoons sherry vinegar
Salt

1½ cups all-purpose flour
1 teaspoon baking powder
1 teaspoon salt
1½ cups grated zucchini
   (1 medium zucchini)
¼ cup sliced scallions,
   plus more for garnishing
   (about 2 scallions)
2 eggs, beaten
1 cup whole milk
Zest of 1 lemon

Preheat the broiler. Set an oven rack 4 inches from the broiler.

To make the romesco:
Place the tomato, cut-side down, on a baking sheet. Drizzle with 1 teaspoon of the olive oil. Broil the tomato until the skin is charred in places and the tomato has softened, about 4 minutes.

Place the tomato, red peppers, garlic, pecans, paprika, and vinegar in a food processor and pulse until combined but not totally pureed. Add the remaining 2 tablespoons olive oil and pulse until smooth. Season with salt.

To make the waffles:
Preheat a waffle iron.

In a bowl, whisk together the flour, baking powder, and salt. In a separate bowl, combine the zucchini, scallions, eggs, milk, and lemon zest. Add the zucchini mixture to the flour mixture and fold together until flour is well incorporated, being careful not to overmix.

Spray the waffle iron with nonstick cooking spray and pour ¾ cup of the batter on the iron. Cook the waffle until golden brown, 3 to 4 minutes. Repeat with the remaining batter.

Sprinkle the waffles with the sliced scallions and serve them with the romesco.

Roasted Carrot Soup *with* Sunflower-Seed Crumble

Yield: 4 to 6 servings   **Prep time:** 25 minutes
Cook time: 40 minutes

Carrots are one of the most versatile and accessible vegetables. And its natural sweetness makes it a kid-friendly offering. They also hold up well under high heat. This crunchy sunflower-seed crumble makes this roasted carrot soup even more delicious.

Sunflower-Seed Crumble:
⅓ cup sunflower seeds (can substitute chopped almonds or pecans)
2 tablespoons old-fashioned rolled oats
2 packed tablespoons chopped pitted dates, ideally soft Medjool (about 2 medium dates)
1 tablespoon melted coconut oil
⅛ teaspoon ground cinnamon
⅛ teaspoon salt, or to taste

1 teaspoon sweet paprika
1 teaspoon ground cumin
⅛ teaspoon ground ginger
⅛ teaspoon ground cinnamon
Salt and freshly ground pepper
8 large carrots (about 2 pounds), trimmed and peeled
1 small or ½ large sweet onion, like Vidalia, chopped
3 tablespoons extra-virgin olive oil
4 to 5 cups low-sodium vegetable or chicken stock, homemade or purchased

To make the crumble:
On a cutting board using a large, sharp knife, chop together the sunflower seeds, oats, and dates until finely chopped and they start to clump together. Transfer to a bowl and stir in the coconut oil, cinnamon, and salt. Mix well.

Preheat the oven to 375°F. Line a baking sheet with parchment paper. Spread the crumble in an even layer and bake, stirring once or twice, until fragrant and lightly browned, 8 to 10 minutes. Transfer to a bowl to cool completely.

To make the soup:
Increase the oven temperature to 425°F. In a bowl, mix together the paprika, cumin, ginger, cinnamon, 1 teaspoon salt, and ¼ teaspoon pepper. Cut the carrots into thick spears, all roughly the same size (halved crosswise, and halved or quartered lengthwise). Arrange the carrots and onion in a single layer on the baking sheet and drizzle with olive oil. Sprinkle with the spice mixture and toss well to combine. Roast until the carrots are very tender and slightly caramelized, turning once or twice, 25 to 30 minutes.

Transfer the carrots to a blender and add 4 cups of the stock (do this in batches if necessary). Puree until very smooth. Transfer to a saucepan. Thin as needed with a little more stock to the consistency you like. Warm over medium-low heat, stirring, until hot. Taste and adjust the seasoning with salt and pepper if needed. Serve in soup bowls, topped with the sunflower seed crumble.

Kelly Carlisle *of* Acta Non Verba Youth Urban Farm Project *in Oakland*

A lemon changed the life of Kelly Carlisle and people all over Oakland. Or, more precisely, a lemon tree. The US Navy veteran was at a nursery buying flowers one day in 2010 when she spotted a little lemon tree. She'd never thought about it before, but in that moment, she wondered, "Could *I* grow a lemon?" She bought the tree to find out.

"I definitely didn't believe I could grow anything, and the next thing I knew, I had grown another two lemons on that tree," Carlisle says. "My mind was blown." That little success inspired her to start a community garden where she could share the experience of growing things and the taste of fresh produce with kids in her East Oakland community.

"When I talk to the kids, I tell them it's a kind of magic, but it's not new," says Carlisle, whose mother is from Atlanta. "It's been withheld and sequestered from normal people. Just growing a couple lemons was really transformational for me and made me realize so much of the bigger picture."

She started telling everyone who would listen that she was looking for a place to start a microfarm. Word got to Cynthia Armstrong, a community activist and director of the Tassafaronga Recreation Center, who was looking to begin a community garden. She took Carlisle to a vacant spot next to a ball field and asked, "Can you work with this?" Carlisle jumped in and named the farm *Acta Non Verba*, which means "deeds, not words" in Latin.

They started out with ten raised beds and soon the garden doubled in size. Now Carlisle, a small staff, volunteers, and students grow crops like arugula, kale, shishito peppers, and strawberries on three different sites. And they've expanded beyond row crops to beehives, flowers like calendula, and a small orchard that includes Pink Lady apples, Cara oranges, and persimmons.

Elementary school kids can enroll in daily after-school farming lessons and earn money toward educational expenses. Besides helping plant, weed, and harvest, they learn regenerative farming techniques like feeding the soil with cover crops and four different ways to compost food scraps. During the four yearly school breaks, ANV Farm offers all-day camps that include archery, art, cooking, and dancing. Besides the regular programming, middle schoolers can join a leadership training program.

The Beet Boxes, a weekly produce subscription that serves three hundred families a week, is their flagship program that reaches outside East Oakland. The boxes are packed with produce grown at Acta Non Verba, plus nuts and grapes from partner BIPOC farmers in the Central Valley and spice mixes from Oakland. This community-supported agriculture program is a win-win: Families know they'll have healthful, fresh produce each week, and it helps the farm fund educational scholarships for kids in the after-school program.

Right now, ANV's gardens are producing at capacity, so Carlisle is on the lookout for a larger parcel nearby. "Our big goal is to find five or more acres of land that we can grow on and where we can hold a sleepaway experience," she says. "We want to be able to really just settle in and know we have control over this piece of land."

During the Covid pandemic in 2020, Acta Non Verba switched to virtual lessons four days a week with in-person farm days on Fridays. But they're still fulfilling their mission. Over the past decade, the program has expanded the palates and minds of more than three thousand kids.

"Everybody eats, and there's a real sense of empowerment that comes when you produce something you can eat, when it's your hands feeding yourself, your family, and your community," Carlisle says.

Stuffed Sweet Potatoes

Yield: 4 servings   **Prep time:** 25 minutes
Cook time: 1 hour

Sweet potatoes are often confused with yams, which are a totally different vegetable. Yams have been a staple of West African communities for thousands of years, beginning in the Niger River basin. When enslaved Africans were brought to the colonies, they substituted sweet potatoes, which were native to the Americas.

2 sweet potatoes, rinsed and patted dry
1 cup cubed (½ inch thick) bread, toasted
½ cup chicken stock, warmed
4 tablespoons unsalted butter (can substitute olive or coconut oil)
¼ cup pancetta, diced small
¼ cup yellow onion, minced
1 tablespoon minced garlic
2 cups finely chopped fresh mustard greens
Salt and freshly ground pepper
3 tablespoons coconut oil
1 tablespoon minced fresh sage
1 tablespoon minced fresh Italian parsley
1 teaspoon minced fresh chives, plus more for garnishing

Gastrique:
½ cup molasses
1 cup apple cider vinegar
Salt and freshly ground pepper

Preheat the oven to 400°F.

Place the whole sweet potatoes on a small sheet pan and bake for 20 minutes. Remove from the oven and let cool.

To make the gastrique:
Combine the molasses and vinegar in a small pot, bring to a boil, and then lower the heat to a simmer. Cook until the liquid thickens and coats the back of a spoon. Season to taste, and keep warm.

Toss the bread and stock together and set aside to hydrate.

In a sauté pan, melt 2 tablespoons of the butter. Add the pancetta and cook until it turns brown and crisp. Add the onion and garlic, then cook until the onion turns soft. Add the mustard greens and sauté until softened. Season with salt and pepper. Set aside.

When the potatoes are cool, slice them in half lengthwise, taking care not to tear their skins. Remove about three-quarters of the flesh, gently dice it, and transfer it to a bowl. Add the coconut oil and toss with the diced potatoes, and season with salt and pepper. Set aside the skins for later use. Place the diced potatoes on a pan and return them to the oven to roast until golden and cooked through. Once the potatoes are cooked, combine with the cooked mustard greens, sage, parsley, and chives in a mixing bowl. Squeeze any excess liquid from the bread croutons and add to the potato mixture. Adjust the seasoning if needed.

Spoon the potato stuffing into the potato skins and dot each one with the remaining 2 tablespoons butter. Place the stuffed potatoes in the oven and cook until the butter melts, 3 to 5 minutes.

Remove the potatoes from the oven, drizzle with gastrique, and sprinkle with chives. Serve warm.

Beluga Lentil Hash

Yield: 8 servings   **Prep time:** 25 minutes
Cook time: 40 minutes

You won't miss the potatoes in this delicious lentil hash. Beluga (also known as black) lentils stay firm but tender, and shine with a classic mirepoix with a little bell pepper thrown in to complete the Creole trinity. Started and finished with butter, my lentil hash is comforting and savory. Top it with a poached egg for a satisfying meal.

4 tablespoons unsalted butter
½ teaspoon cayenne pepper
1 small yellow onion, diced
1 large or 2 small carrots, peeled and diced
2 stalks celery, diced
1 small red bell pepper, seeded and diced
Salt and freshly ground black pepper
3 sprigs fresh thyme
1½ cups beluga lentils, picked and rinsed
4½ cups vegetable broth
1 tablespoon Louisiana-style hot sauce
8 eggs
2 tablespoons chopped fresh chives, plus more for garnishing
2 tablespoons chopped fresh Italian parsley, plus more for garnishing

In a large skillet, heat 2 tablespoons of the butter over medium-high heat. Add the cayenne pepper, onion, carrot, celery, and bell pepper. Sauté until the vegetables turn tender and start to brown, about 6 minutes. Season with salt and black pepper and add the thyme. Add the lentils and broth and bring to a simmer. Lower the heat and let simmer, stirring occasionally, until the lentils are tender and the liquid is mostly absorbed but the lentils are still moist, 15 to 20 minutes. Remove from the heat, stir in the remaining 2 tablespoons of butter and hot sauce, and stir until the butter is melted.

In a medium skillet, add water to a depth of about 3 inches. Generously salt the water and bring to a boil over medium-high heat, then lower the heat to a bare simmer. Carefully break four of the eggs, one at a time, and slip them into the water, taking care not to crowd the pan. Cook until the whites are set and the yolks are still runny, about 3 minutes. With a slotted spoon, transfer the eggs to a kitchen towel to drain. Repeat with the remaining four eggs.

Stir the 2 tablespoons chives and parsley into the lentils and season with salt and pepper. Spoon the hash onto eight plates. Top each plate with a poached egg. Garnish with more parsley and chives.

New Orleans Barbecued Black Cod

Yield: 4 servings   **Prep time:** 5 minutes
Cook time: 15 minutes

Black cod is one of the most succulent and satisfying fish ever, and it's easy to make at home. The key is to sear it so that it gets a nice crust; just be careful not to overcook it! The sauce reminds me of a mashup between what you might find on New Orleans shrimp and the miso cod that the renowned restaurant Nobu made famous. The Worcestershire sauce supplies the umami that normally comes from miso. Sop up this NOLa beurre blanc with some crusty bread.

Four 6-ounce black cod fillets
1½ tablespoons Creole seasoning
2 tablespoons extra-virgin olive oil
¼ cup Worcestershire sauce
¼ cup chicken broth
Juice of 1 lemon
8 tablespoons cold unsalted butter, cut into cubes
3 scallions, thinly sliced
Crusty bread for serving

Preheat the oven to 400°F.

Season the cod generously with ¾ tablespoon of the Creole seasoning. Heat the olive oil in a sauté pan over medium-high heat. Add the cod, flesh-side down, and cook until golden brown, about 3 minutes. Turn the cod over and cook until the skin is golden brown, another 2 minutes. Transfer the cod from the pan to a baking sheet. Place in the oven and bake just until cooked through, about 4 more minutes.

To the sauté pan, add the remaining ¾ tablespoon Creole seasoning, Worcestershire sauce, chicken broth, and lemon juice. Cook over medium heat, scraping the bottom of the pan, until the sauce is reduced by one-third, 2 to 3 minutes. Lower the heat and start adding the butter, a few cubes at a time, and swirl the pan to melt the butter. Add a few more cubes once the first few have melted, and continue until the butter is incorporated and the sauce is smooth and emulsified. Stir in all but 2 tablespoons of the scallions.

Remove the cod from the oven and place on four plates or a platter. Pour the sauce over the cod. Sprinkle with the remaining 2 tablespoons scallions and serve with crusty bread to sop up the sauce.

Braised Chicken Thighs *with* Barbecued White Beans *and* Scallions

Yield: 4 to 6 servings   **Prep time:** 20 minutes
Cook time: 1 hour 10 minutes

Flavor fans know that chicken thighs are the tastiest part of the bird. Braising allows this succulent meat to break down, so it literally falls off the bone! Piling this juicy chicken atop a bowl of smoky white beans means you won't miss a bit of flavor. Serve this on a chilly fall night with a glass of Pinot Noir and some soothing jazz, and you'll have yourself a whole vibe. If you're short on time, you can substitute 1 cup of store-bought barbecue sauce thinned with ½ cup of chicken broth.

Barbecue Sauce:
½ cup chicken broth, vegetable stock, or beer
1 cup diced or crushed tomatoes
2 tablespoons tomato paste
3 tablespoons apple cider vinegar
3 tablespoons Worcestershire sauce
2 tablespoons brown sugar
1 tablespoon dark molasses (optional)
1 tablespoon coarse-grain or brown mustard

4 to 6 bone-in, skin-on chicken thighs
Salt and freshly ground pepper
6 slices bacon
2 tablespoons neutral oil, such as avocado or grapeseed

Season the chicken all over with salt and pepper and set aside.

To make the barbecue sauce:
In a small saucepan, combine the chicken broth, tomatoes, tomato paste, vinegar, Worcestershire sauce, sugar, molasses if using, and mustard, and whisk to combine. Bring to a simmer over medium heat and cook until fragrant, about 2 minutes. Set aside.

In a 12-inch ovenproof skillet with a lid (cast-iron is great) over medium heat, fry the bacon until the fat renders and it is crisp. Transfer the bacon to a paper towel to drain, leaving the fat in the pan. Discard all but 2 tablespoons fat (or add oil so you have about 2 tablespoons in the pan). Increase the heat to medium-high. Add the chicken, skin-side down, and sear until well browned, about 5 minutes. Turn and brown the other side, about 3 minutes. Transfer the chicken to a plate.

Preheat the oven to 350°F.

Pour out all but 2 tablespoons of the fat from the pan. Reduce the heat to medium and add the onion, bell pepper, celery, and

continued

1 small yellow onion,
  finely chopped
1 small bell pepper (green,
  red, or a mixture),
  stemmed, seeded, and
  finely chopped
1 stalk celery, finely chopped
2 large garlic cloves, minced
½ teaspoon crushed red
  pepper flakes or ½ jalapeño
  chile, minced
3 cups cooked white beans
  (from 1 heaping cup dried
  beans or two 15-ounce
  cans, drained and rinsed)
⅓ cup chicken broth,
  vegetable stock, or beer
2 or 3 scallions, thinly sliced
Fresh Italian parsley,
  chopped

a pinch of salt. Cook, stirring, until the vegetables become tender, about 5 minutes. Add the garlic and red pepper flakes and stir to combine. Stir in the beans and reserved bacon. Set aside ½ cup of the barbecue sauce and add the rest to the bean mixture along with the chicken broth. Bring the mixture to a boil, lower the heat to medium-low, cover the pan, and let simmer, stirring occasionally, for 5 minutes.

Return the chicken to the pan, skin-side up. Cover the pan and transfer to the oven. Cook until the chicken is cooked through, about 30 minutes. Let sit for 5 minutes. Sprinkle with the scallions and parsley and serve, passing the reserved barbecue sauce alongside.

Apple Cider-Brined Pork Chops *with* Country Fried Apples

Yield: 4 servings   **Prep time:** 30 minutes, plus 30 minutes for brine cooling and 4 to 24 hours for brining
Cook time: 45 minutes

Pork chops and apples is a longtime comfort cuisine classic, but this version looks at this familiar pairing in a whole new way. This brine has the perfect balance of acid, sugar, and salt. Searing the apples in a cast-iron skillet gives them texture, and the cider glaze ties the whole dish together.

Apple-Cider Brine:
2 cups water
¼ cup salt
¼ cup maple syrup
7 bay leaves
1 tablespoon cracked pepper
4 cups apple cider, chilled

2 teaspoons onion powder
2 teaspoons garlic powder
Four 1½-inch-thick, bone-in
   pork chops
2 tablespoons olive oil
3 tablespoons unsalted butter
3 Granny Smith apples,
   cored and sliced into
   ¼-inch-thick slices, skin on
Salt and freshly ground
   black pepper

To make the brine:

Heat the water in a small saucepan over medium heat. Add the salt, maple syrup, three of the bay leaves, and the cracked pepper and stir until the salt is totally dissolved. Remove from the heat and add the cold apple cider. Cool to room temperature.

Place the brine in a resealable bag or baking pan. Add the pork chops and make sure they are submerged in the brine. Refrigerate for at least 4 hours and up to 24 hours. Preheat the oven to 425°F.

Add the onion and garlic powders, and the remaining four bay leaves to a spice grinder. Grind to a fine powder. Remove the chops from the brine and pat dry. Reserve 1 cup of the brine. Coat the chops with the spice mix.

In a large cast-iron pan, heat the olive oil over medium-high heat. Add two of the chops and cook until golden brown, about 4 minutes. Flip the chops and cook until golden on the other side, 2 more minutes. Transfer to a baking sheet and repeat with the remaining two pork chops. Place the chops in the oven and cook until they reach 145°F on an instant-read thermometer, about 15 minutes. Remove from the oven and let rest for 10 minutes.

In a cast-iron pan, heat 1½ tablespoons butter over medium-high heat. Add half the apples, season with salt and pepper, and cook on one side until golden brown, about 2 minutes. Flip and cook until golden brown. Transfer to a plate and repeat with the remaining 1½ tablespoons butter and the remaining apples. Remove the apples and add the reserved 1 cup brine to the pan. Bring to a simmer and cook until reduced by two-thirds, about 6 minutes.

Serve the chops topped with apples and the reduced brine.

Rob Archie *of* Urban Roots Brewery *and* Smokehouse *in Sacramento*

Basketball led Rob Archie to beer and to running a craft brewery and restaurant. But not the way you think.

Growing up near Sacramento, Archie was a tall kid who liked to shoot hoops. His talents as a shooting guard took him to San Diego State University, where he played basketball while earning a degree in criminal justice.

Before starting his career as a social worker, Archie spent a year playing basketball in Europe. He loved living in Rome, right around the corner from the Vatican. Going to the neighborhood coffee bar became a favorite daily ritual. He liked the way the barista made his macchiato or cappuccino. Then he pauses. "He was patient enough for you to enjoy it while you were in front of him," Archie says. He started going to the same place every morning. He realized all the clientele knew one another.

"This is how they start the morning, and this is how they connect. All of a sudden, you feel a part of a community. I never felt that before," Archie says. "I was like, that's what's needed in the States. We need to build more community."

Also, we needed better beer. "We're in America, and this is the greatest country, but we've been domesticated on bad beer," Archie declares. He was still working his 9-to-5 job and running a nonprofit to help student athletes excel academically when he opened Pangea, his first beer-focused restaurant. He started going to Belgium to curate beers and dreamed of brewing his own.

Starting a brewery, which requires buying and storing large quantities of barley and hops, as well as setting up massive vats for boiling and huge fermenting tanks, might seem daunting. But Archie says his grandfather, who was from Louisiana, and his dad taught him about industry. His dad started a trucking business as a teenager, hauling peaches, tomatoes, pears, rice, barley, and wheat— all the crops growing around the Sacramento Delta. "That's how I learned what our region was about," Archie says. "We would go to canneries with loads of tomatoes and see manufacturing on a large scale. That exposed me to what hard work is."

In 2018, he teamed with brewer Peter Hoey to open Urban Roots Brewery & Smokehouse so they could create their own craft brews and serve it up with barbecue. Just like in old-school German beer halls, they have long tables, where he says you'll find lovers, families, friends, and neighbors gathering over beers like Perpetual Journey saison, Be More Kind IPA, and Chocolate Moustache imperial dessert stout. He's proud of the community he's built.

"Beer is the ultimate social lubricant for social intercourse," says Archie. "It's a communal beverage. Good people drink good beer."

Whole Duck Jambalaya *with* Confit Duck Legs

Yield: 6 servings

Confit	**Prep time:** 15 minutes, plus overnight cure	**Cook time:** 3 hours, plus cooling time
Jambalaya	**Prep time:** 25 minutes	**Cook time:** 50 minutes

Jambalaya is a Southern favorite that's a direct descendant of West African jollof rice. Africans from Senegal and Sierra Leone were enslaved and brought to the Carolina coast and the Georgia Sea Islands to cultivate rice in America. By the 1800s, rice was a dominant crop in California, and it's still prevalent today. I love buying local whenever possible and fortunately, Liberty Duck Farms is right "up the street" in Sonoma County. Their ducks are raised sustainably, and luckily, the company ships nationally.

Confit Duck Legs:

1 whole duck
1 tablespoon salt
4 garlic cloves
2 bay leaves
6 sprigs fresh thyme
3 cups duck fat, melted

1 small yellow onion, diced
2 stalks celery, chopped
1 bell pepper, stemmed, seeded, and chopped
2 teaspoons Creole seasoning
2 garlic cloves, chopped
1 cup chopped tomatoes (optional)
2 teaspoons Worcestershire sauce
1 teaspoon Louisiana-style hot sauce
2 cups long-grain white rice
4 cups chicken broth
2 scallions, thinly sliced

To make the confit:

Remove the legs from the duck. Carefully cut the breasts from the duck and trim off excess fat. Cover the duck breasts and refrigerate.

Sprinkle the duck legs with salt all over, and place them in a small baking pan. In a food processor, combine the garlic, bay leaves, and thyme and process until finely chopped. Rub the herb mixture over the duck legs to evenly coat them. Cover the pan and refrigerate overnight.

Preheat the oven to 250°F.

Remove the pan of duck legs from the refrigerator. Pour the melted duck fat over the legs so it submerges them. Cover the pan with aluminum foil and bake until the legs are cooked and tender, about 3 hours. Remove from the oven and let cool to room temperature. Pull the meat off the bones, discarding the skin and bones but reserving some of the liquid fat. Roughly chop the meat and set aside.

continued

To make the jambalaya:

Heat 2 tablespoons of the reserved duck fat in a Dutch oven over medium heat. Add the onion, celery, bell pepper, and Creole seasoning and cook until tender but not brown, about 6 minutes. Add the garlic, tomatoes if using, Worcestershire sauce, and hot sauce and cook for 1 minute. Stir in the rice, broth, and the reserved duck confit. Bring to a simmer, cover, and cook until the rice is tender, about 20 minutes. Turn off the heat and let sit, still covered, for 10 minutes.

Meanwhile, cook the duck breasts. Carefully cut diagonal lines every ½ inch across the fat without cutting down to the meat. Then cut lines in the opposite direction to make a diamond pattern. Season both sides of both duck breasts with salt and pepper.

Place the duck breasts in a cold cast-iron pan, fat-side down. Turn the heat on low and let the breasts cook without moving them as the fat renders out, 12 to 15 minutes. Once the fat is deep golden brown and most of it has been rendered, raise the heat to medium-high, turn the breasts over, and cook for 2 to 4 minutes, just until browned and the temperature reaches 130°F on an instant-read thermometer.

Remove the duck breasts from the heat and let sit for 10 minutes.

Stir in all but 2 tablespoons of the scallions into the jambalaya. Slice the duck breasts and place on top of the jambalaya. Sprinkle with the remaining scallions.

Chocolate Hazelnut Thumbprint Cookies

Yield: 3 dozen cookies **Prep time:** 25 minutes, plus 30 minutes of dough chilling
Cook time: 25 minutes

Hazelnut trees grow wild across California and the western United States, bearing fruit in the autumn. That's why these intensely flavored nuts are often a part of Thanksgiving and harvest season meals. I first discovered them while cooking in France, where they're a common ingredient in savory and sweet dishes.

¾ cup hazelnuts
½ cup granulated sugar
8 tablespoons unsalted
  butter, room temperature
1 egg
1½ cups all-purpose flour,
  plus more for dusting
1 teaspoon fine sea salt
1 teaspoon vanilla extract

Ganache:
1 cup bittersweet chocolate
  chips
¼ cup heavy cream

Flaky sea salt

Preheat the oven to 350°F.

Toast the hazelnuts on a small baking sheet in the oven just until they turn fragrant, 8 to 10 minutes. Watch them so they don't burn. Remove the hazelnuts from the oven and while they're still hot, rub them in a kitchen towel to remove as many of their skins as possible; it's okay if a few skins remain. Allow to cool.

Add the hazelnuts to a food processor along with the sugar. Pulse until they are finely ground and they have a similar texture to the sugar. Add the butter and pulse until well combined. Add the egg and pulse until well combined. Add the flour, fine sea salt, and vanilla and pulse until a dough is formed. Turn the dough out onto a lightly floured surface and pat into a disc. Wrap with plastic wrap and refrigerate for at least 30 minutes. Preheat the oven to 350°F.

Form the dough into 1- to 1½-inch balls and place them 1 inch apart on a baking sheet. Press your thumb down in the center of each ball to create an indent in the dough.

Bake the cookies until golden brown and just set, 12 to 15 minutes. Transfer the cookies to a wire rack and cool completely.

To make the ganache:
Place the chocolate chips in a small bowl. In a small saucepan, bring the cream to a simmer over low heat. Pour the cream over the chocolate and let sit for 1 minute. Stir to fully melt the chocolate. Cool.

Transfer the ganache to a piping bag or a resealable plastic bag with the end snipped off. Pipe the ganache into the indentations in the cooled cookies. Sprinkle the cookies with flaky sea salt.

Gravenstein Apple Hand Pies

Yield: 8 hand pies   **Prep time:** 40 minutes, plus 30 minutes to 12 hours of dough chilling
Cook time: 30 minutes

Sonoma County is the lesser-known wine country, but it's so much more. It's nestled along the coast on the west side and brimming with farmland on the east side. Tart green Gravenstein apples are grown all over. These mini-pies are a smart way to use up leftover dough and filling, and thrift is a core tenet of the African-American kitchen.

Dough:
2¼ cups all-purpose flour, plus more for dusting
1 cup unsalted butter, cut into cubes and chilled
1 teaspoon salt
4 to 7 tablespoons ice water

Filling:
2 Gravenstein apples (about 1 pound), peeled, cored, and diced ¼ inch thick
¼ teaspoon ground allspice
1 teaspoon ground cinnamon
2 tablespoons granulated sugar
½ teaspoon salt
1 tablespoon tapioca starch

⅓ cup apple butter
1 egg, lightly beaten

Glaze:
1 cup confectioners' sugar
2 tablespoons apple cider

Combine the flour, butter, and salt in a food processor and pulse until the mixture resembles small peas. Add 4 tablespoons of the ice water and pulse just until the dough holds together when pressed between your fingers. If necessary, add more ice water, 1 tablespoon at a time. Be careful not to overprocess.

Turn the dough out onto a lightly floured surface and press lightly to form a disk. Wrap with plastic wrap and refrigerate for at least 30 minutes or up to overnight.

Preheat the oven to 350°F.

Line a sheet pan with a silicone mat or parchment paper. Toss together the apples, allspice, cinnamon, sugar, salt, and tapioca starch.

On a lightly floured surface, roll out the dough into an 18-inch circle, ⅛ inch thick. Cut into twelve 4-inch circles. Gather and reroll the scraps to get four more circles for a total of sixteen. Spread 1 teaspoon of the apple butter in the center of eight of the dough circles, leaving a ½-inch border. Place ¼ cup of the filling on top of the apple butter. Brush the edge of the dough with the egg and top with a plain dough circle. Using a fork, seal the edges of the dough of each pie. Cut three slits into the top of each pie and place the pies on the prepared sheet pan. Refrigerate for 20 minutes.

Brush the pies with the remaining egg and bake until golden brown, 25 to 30 minutes.

To make the glaze:
Whisk together the confectioners' sugar and apple cider in a small bowl until the sugar is dissolved. Drizzle the glaze onto the hand pies and let cool.

Fresh Gingerbread Cupcakes *with* Molasses Buttercream

Yield: 12 cupcakes   **Prep time:** 25 minutes
Cook time: 25 minutes

Thick brown molasses is central to Southern soul food, where it was once a prized sweetener saved for special occasions. But its sweetness is tinged with sadness too, as it is a by-product of the sugar production that drove the transatlantic slave trade. Molasses adds a distinct, earthy sweetness to this buttercream, which makes the gingerbread shine.

2 cups all-purpose flour
2 teaspoons baking powder
1 teaspoon fine sea salt
½ teaspoon ground cinnamon
¼ teaspoon ground cloves
¼ teaspoon ground allspice
¼ teaspoon ground nutmeg
⅛ teaspoon freshly ground pepper
2 eggs
½ cup granulated sugar
½ cup firmly packed dark brown sugar
1 tablespoon molasses
⅓ cup vegetable oil
2 teaspoons finely grated fresh ginger
¾ cup whole milk

Molasses Buttercream:

1 cup unsalted butter, room temperature
¼ cup molasses
3 cups confectioners' sugar
2 tablespoons heavy cream
1 pinch fine sea salt

To make the cupcakes:

Preheat the oven to 350°F. Line a twelve-well cupcake tin with cupcake liners or spray with nonstick cooking spray.

In a medium bowl, whisk together the flour, baking powder, salt, cinnamon, cloves, allspice, nutmeg, and pepper.

Using a stand mixer fitted with the paddle attachment, mix the eggs, granulated sugar, brown sugar, molasses, vegetable oil, and ginger on medium speed until well combined, scraping down the sides of the mixer with a spatula. Add the flour mixture and milk in three intervals, starting and ending with the flour. Mix until smooth.

Using an ice cream scoop, fill each well three-quarters full of batter. Bake until a toothpick inserted in the center comes out clean, 20 to 25 minutes. Remove the cupcakes from the oven and let sit for 5 minutes. Transfer them to a wire rack to cool completely.

To make the buttercream:

Using a stand mixer with a whisk attachment, mix the butter and molasses on medium speed until light and fluffy, about 3 minutes. Add the confectioners' sugar and mix on low speed until well incorporated, scraping down the sides of the mixer with a spatula. Add the cream and salt and beat on medium speed until smooth, about 3 minutes.

Transfer the buttercream to a piping bag or a resealable plastic bag with the end snipped off. Pipe the frosting onto the cupcakes. Alternately, spread the frosting with a small offset spatula.

California Date Bars

Yield: 24 bars   **Prep time:** 30 minutes, plus 15 minutes of date cooling and 30 minutes of dough chilling
Cook time: 30 minutes

Date palms are native to North Africa and the Middle East, but they've thrived in California since the late 1600s, when Spanish priests planted them as they established missions across the state. The intense sweetness of dates makes them a great substitute for honey or sugar.

1½ cups Medjool dates, pitted
1 cup water
1 teaspoon vanilla paste or extract
2 teaspoons salt
2½ cups all-purpose flour
1 teaspoon baking powder
1 teaspoon ground cinnamon
1 cup unsalted butter, room temperature
½ cup firmly packed dark brown sugar
¼ cup honey
2 eggs

In a saucepan, combine the dates with the water and bring to a simmer over medium-high heat. Turn off the heat and let sit for 15 minutes. Strain the water from the dates, reserving the liquid. Add the dates to a food processor with the vanilla paste, 1 teaspoon of the salt, and ¼ cup of the reserved date water. Process until smooth, adding 1 tablespoon of additional date water at a time if the mixture is too thick—it should be the texture of a thick jam.

Line a 9 by 13-inch baking pan with parchment paper so the paper hangs over the sides of the pan. This will make it easy to lift the bars out of the pan once they're baked. Spray the parchment with nonstick cooking spray.

In a bowl, whisk together the flour, baking powder, the remaining 1 teaspoon salt, and cinnamon. Using a stand mixer fitted with a paddle attachment, add the butter, brown sugar, and honey and mix on medium speed until well combined, about 2 minutes, scraping down the sides of the mixer with a spatula. Add the eggs, one at a time, mixing until incorporated. Turn off the mixer and add the flour mixture. Mix on low speed until the flour is fully incorporated, scraping down the sides as necessary with a spatula. The dough will be soft. Place half of the dough in the prepared pan and spread evenly with an offset spatula. Carefully spread the date mixture evenly over the top of the dough in the pan. Place the pan in the freezer for 30 minutes. Preheat the oven to 350°F.

Remove the pan from the freezer. Take the remaining half of the dough, place dollops of it over the top of the date mixture in the pan, and carefully spread it evenly over the date layer. Bake until the top is golden brown, about 30 minutes. Let cool for 15 minutes.

Using the parchment paper, lift the bars out of the pan and place on a wire rack to cool. Cut into twenty-four squares.

Alma de Oakland

Yield: 1 cocktail

Oakland is a vibrant city full of people from many different backgrounds and food traditions. My city's diversity is what keeps life here exciting. I have so much gratitude and respect for our large Latinx community and the many people from across Latin America who have worked with me and become friends. This cocktail is a nod to them. And our work together has cemented my appreciation for the diversity of the Hispanic cultures.

Tajín
Ice
2 ounces Mix (recipe follows)
2¼ ounces Batch
   (recipe follows)
Lime slice for garnishing

Mix:
3 ounces lime juice
3 ounces Chile Orgeat
   (see below)
2 ounces Simple Syrup
   (see below)

Batch:
1 ounce Amaro Nonino
1 ounce Pimm's No. 1
1 ounce reposado tequila
2 ounces brandy
4 ounces blanco tequila

Chile Orgeat:
1½ cups good-quality
   almond milk
1 cup Demerara or
   brown sugar
3 to 4 slices jalapeño chile

Simple Syrup:
1 cup granulated sugar
1 cup water

Pour some Tajín on a plate. Dab the rim of a cocktail glass in the Tajín to coat. Fill the glass with ice.

Combine the mix and batch in a cocktail shaker and shake vigorously for 10 seconds. Strain into the prepared glass, garnish with a lime slice, and serve.

In a medium pot, heat the almond milk over medium-high heat. Reduce by one-third, then add the sugar and jalapeño. Stir until the sugar is dissolved. Remove from the heat, let cool, and strain. This mixture can be stored in the refrigerator for up to 1 week.

To make the simple syrup:
Bring the water and sugar to a boil and stir. Once the sugar is dissolved, turn off the heat and cool.

WINTER

Winter Chicory Salad *with* Blood Oranges, Pomegranates, *and* Creole Mustard Vinaigrette

Yield: 6 servings   **Prep time:** 20 minutes

Coffee connoisseurs know chicory as a bitter root that's a popular coffee substitute and medicinal drink in South Africa. This roasted root gives Café du Monde's famous New Orleans coffee its signature flavors. But above ground, this cousin of the dandelion sprouts a bitter green that's rich in potassium and magnesium. A soulful Creole mustard vinaigrette ties the greens, blood oranges, and pomegranates together.

3 blood oranges
1 pound mixed chicories
  (such as radicchio,
  escarole, or endive), torn
  into bite-size pieces
¼ cup coarsely chopped
  roasted almonds
¼ cup pomegranate seeds
2 tablespoons chopped
  chives

**Creole Mustard
Vinaigrette:**
1 tablespoon Creole mustard
1 teaspoon honey
2 tablespoons champagne
  vinegar
¼ cup extra-virgin olive oil
Salt and freshly ground
  pepper

Cut off the tops and bottoms of the oranges to expose their flesh. Rest one orange on one of its cut sides and carefully slice down the side, following the orange's curve to fully expose the flesh and remove its skin and pith. Once all the skin and pith are removed, hold the orange over a small bowl and carefully cut in between the segments to release its supremes, or segments. Reserve these supremes in a separate bowl and let the excess juice drip into the small bowl. Once all the supremes are collected, squeeze the remaining pulp into the small bowl. Repeat with the other two oranges. You should now have about 2 tablespoons of juice in the bowl.

To make the vinaigrette:
Add the mustard, honey, and vinegar to the orange juice and whisk to combine. While whisking, drizzle in the olive oil. Season with salt and pepper.

Place the chicories in a bowl or on a platter. Sprinkle with the almonds, pomegranate seeds, reserved orange supremes, and chives. Drizzle with the vinaigrette and toss well.

Keba Konte *of* Red Bay Coffee *in Oakland*

Being open to new experiences and immersing himself in his passions led Keba Konte to where he is now: diversifying the coffee business with Red Bay Coffee, the label that he imports and sells in his burgeoning chain of coffeehouses.

From an early age, Konte says he believed that he'd work for himself. "In college I knew I'd be an entrepreneur. I just didn't know what I wanted to do."

Konte was born in 1966, in San Francisco's Haight-Ashbury district, where the streets were filled with flower children and protests. His father was from Georgia and his mother was from Florida. They met in the Bay Area and settled in the heart of the city.

His parents were activists, and they appreciated fine food and drinks. His mother Pam was a coffee lover, and he remembers the aroma filling his home growing up as she made coffee. They'd go to North Beach so she could buy her favorite beans from Graffeo Coffee. "My first coffee impressions were exposure from my mom, like most of the things that are worthwhile when you're young," he says. "I remember going to this place with this overwhelming smell and a bunch of grumpy old Italian guys. That was very gourmet at the time. It wasn't a bad smell. It was a lot. It was intense," he says.

As a student and a wrestler at San Francisco State University, he started drinking Peet's Coffee, a seminal Bay Area brand that favored a deeply roasted flavor profile. "I was drinking lattes; what's not to like about a latte: the caffeine, the mother's milk, and sugar?" In college he became passionate about photography, a passion that changed the course of his life. He decided to leave school and went to South Africa to photograph Nelson Mandela's 1984 inauguration.

That life-changing South Africa experience propelled him into a career as a professional photographer. He shot all kinds of subjects, but he became known for working with Bay Area hip-hop artists, including E-40, Master P, Richie Rich, and the Conscious Daughters.

Then Konte found that he was drawn to fine art. He specialized in mixed-media pieces, which might include found objects, copper, and leather, and he had the opportunity to travel the world to exhibit his work. "And then coffee snuck in through the back door," he says.

An artist friend offered Konte and his wife Rachel the opportunity to start a café at the site of Smokey Joe's, one of the first vegan restaurants in the state. Guerrilla Café was the place to go for vegan waffles served with an international activist vibe. He's proud to note they were the first spot to pour Blue Bottle coffee.

The Red Bay slogan "Beautiful Coffee to the People" speaks to the team's work to make sure everyone is welcome, whether they're at their Ferry Building location in San Francisco, the East Oakland locale where the beans are roasted, or its airy headquarters in Oakland's Fruitvale neighborhood with its soaring ceilings and a mid-century vibe seen in George Nelson pendant lights and low Risom chairs.

Visit any one of his coffee shops, and you'll see and hear a little of everything Konte loves: black-and-white photography, mixed-media artwork, international textiles, fresh R&B soundtracks, and trendsetting drinks, like their inky charcoal latte, which satisfies and cleanses at the same time.

Dungeness Crab Beignets

Yield: 24 beignets   **Prep time:** 25 minutes
Cook time: 20 minutes

Nothing says New Orleans like a beignet (pronounced ben-YAY).
Sprinkled with confectioners' sugar, the sweet version of these pillows
of airy dough is popular. But I think you'll agree that this savory
version, with buttery Dungeness crab, is next level. The sweet lemon
salt highlights the sweetness of the crab and ties them to the classic
version. The splash of sparkling wine in the batter makes these super-
light, and you'll have plenty left over to sip with your beignets.

Sweet Lemon Salt:

1 tablespoon lemon zest
 (from 1 large or 2 small
 lemons)
2 tablespoons confectioners'
 sugar
1 teaspoon salt

1 tablespoon olive oil
1 tablespoon unsalted butter
½ small onion, finely diced
½ green bell pepper,
 finely diced
1 stalk celery, finely diced
1 teaspoon Old Bay
 seasoning
Salt and freshly ground
 black pepper
1 garlic clove, chopped
Vegetable oil for frying
1 cup all-purpose flour
1½ teaspoons baking powder
½ teaspoon fine sea salt
1 egg, beaten
½ cup dry sparkling wine
 (or seltzer)

8 ounces Dungeness lump
 crabmeat
Lemon Aioli (page 197)

To make the lemon salt:
Place the lemon zest on a plate in an even layer and microwave for
2 to 2½ minutes, just to dry it out a little. Let cool. Combine the
zest, sugar, and salt in a spice grinder and grind until powdery.
Set aside.

In a sauté pan, heat the olive oil and butter over medium-high
heat. Add the onion, bell pepper, and celery and season with Old
Bay seasoning, salt, and black pepper. Sauté until the vegetables
are soft and translucent but not browning, about 4 minutes. Add
the garlic and cook 30 seconds more. Remove from the heat and
allow to cool.

Heat 4 inches of vegetable oil in a deep pot to 325°F.

In a large bowl, whisk together the flour, baking powder, and
sea salt. Stir in the egg and sparkling wine and mix just until the
mixture is combined and mostly smooth. Gently fold in the cooled
vegetables and the crabmeat.

Line a plate with paper towels. Using a tablespoon or small
scoop, carefully add the batter to the oil in batches, being careful
not to crowd the pot. Fry until golden brown, about 3 minutes.
Transfer the beignets to the prepared plate to drain, and season
with the lemon salt. Serve immediately with lemon aioli.

Dungeness Crab Salad *with* Cornmeal-Crusted Green Tomatoes, Honey-Pickled Shallots, *and* Lemon Aioli

Yield: 4 servings   **Prep time:** 25 minutes
Cook time: 5 minutes

Blue crabs rule out East, but on the West Coast, it's all about the Dungeness crab. My ancestors probably enjoyed fiddler crabs in West Africa or the small blue crabs found along the Eastern Seaboard. We love Dungeness crabs because they're so big, which makes picking out the meat a snap. Green tomatoes fried with a cornmeal crust create the perfect vehicle for this crab salad. Make the aioli in the blender so it's super-fast and convenient.

Honey-Pickled Shallots:
1 tablespoon champagne
   vinegar
2 teaspoons honey
1 small shallot, thinly sliced

Lemon Aioli:
1 egg yolk
2 tablespoons lemon juice
1 tablespoon lemon zest
1 garlic clove, chopped
1 pinch cayenne pepper
½ cup neutral oil, such as
   grapeseed or vegetable
2 tablespoons California
   extra-virgin olive oil
Salt

To make the shallots:
In a small bowl, whisk together the vinegar and honey. Add the sliced shallots, mix well, and set aside.

To make the aioli:
Add the egg yolk, lemon juice and zest, garlic, and cayenne pepper to a blender. Turn on the blender and slowly drizzle in the neutral oil and olive oil. If the mixture gets too thick, thin with a few drops of water. Season with salt and set aside.

Place the tomato slices on paper towels and pat very dry. Place the flour in a shallow bowl and season generously with salt and pepper. Break the eggs into another shallow bowl, season with salt and pepper, and mix well. Place the cornmeal in a third shallow bowl, season with salt and pepper, and mix well. In two or three batches, dredge the tomato slices in the flour, shaking off excess flour. Dredge the tomato slices in the egg and then the cornmeal, making sure they are well coated.

continued

2 large green tomatoes, cored and sliced ¼ inch thick (8 slices total or 12 if the tomatoes are smaller)

1 cup all-purpose flour

Freshly ground black pepper

2 eggs

1 cup medium- or coarse-grind cornmeal

Vegetable oil for frying

8 ounces picked Dungeness crabmeat

1 tablespoon chopped fresh tarragon

1 tablespoon chopped fresh chives, plus more for garnishing

Place a wire rack over a sheet pan. Heat ½ inch of vegetable oil in a skillet over medium-high heat. If the oil sizzles when you sprinkle in a little flour, it is ready. Add a few tomato slices at a time and pan-fry until golden brown on both sides, about 1 minute per side. Transfer to the rack and season immediately with salt.

Toss the crabmeat with 3 tablespoons of the aioli, tarragon, chives, and 1 tablespoon of the pickled shallots. Season with salt and pepper.

Place a smear of the remaining aioli on each of four plates. Place two fried tomato slices on top of each smear. Top the tomatoes with one-quarter of the crab salad. Drizzle with the remaining aioli, sprinkle with chives, and garnish with the remaining shallots.

Root Vegetable Puree

Yield: 4 to 6 servings (about 3½ cups)   **Prep time:** 10 minutes
Cook time: 25 minutes

Root vegetables have been the staple for Black chefs for centuries.
The texture of this puree resembles fufu, a foundational West African
dish made from ground cassava, plantain, or malanga root. The vanilla
may throw you off, but here it adds a subtle fragrance that elevates
the natural sweetness of the root vegetables. I like to serve this dish
as a side to a richly flavored meat, such as oxtail, lamb, or goat.

4 medium parsnips
  (1 pound), peeled and
  cut into 2-inch chunks
1 medium rutabaga
  (1 pound), peeled and
  cut into 2-inch chunks
Salt
¼ cup heavy cream
3 tablespoons unsalted butter
2 teaspoons vanilla extract

Place the parsnips and rutabaga in a large saucepot. Cover
by at least 2 inches of cold water. Add 1 tablespoon salt to the
water and bring to a boil over medium-high heat. Cook until
the parsnips and rutabaga are tender when pierced with a fork,
20 to 25 minutes. Drain.

Add the parsnips and rutabaga to a food processor. Add the
cream, butter, and vanilla and puree until very smooth. Season
with salt.

Coconut Creamed Dinosaur Kale

Yield: 4 to 6 servings (2¾ cups)   **Prep time:** 20 minutes
Cook time: 20 minutes

One of the most beloved and musically named Caribbean dishes is callaloo. While it varies from island to island, it always includes fresh bitter greens, herbs, and hot peppers in coconut milk. This is a riff on that dish and I use an immersion blender to make this an easy one-pot side dish. I like it a bit chunky, but you can puree it to your desired consistency. I also prefer to not overcook the kale, as I think the added texture gives this dish an edge over creamed spinach.

2 tablespoons coconut oil
1 small yellow onion, thinly sliced
3 garlic cloves, thinly sliced
1 Calabrian chile, coarsely chopped
3 bunches dinosaur or lacinato kale, stems removed and roughly torn into large pieces (about 1½ pounds total or 12 cups)
One 13½-ounce can unsweetened coconut milk, shaken
Salt and freshly ground pepper

In a large saucepan, heat the coconut oil over medium-high heat. Add the onion and cook until softened, 3 to 4 minutes. Add the garlic and Calabrian chile and cook for 1 minute. Add half of the kale and cook until it has wilted down a bit, about 2 minutes. Add the remaining kale and 3 tablespoons of the coconut milk and cook, stirring, until the kale is fully wilted and tender, 6 to 7 minutes. Add the remaining coconut milk, bring to a simmer, and cook until the kale is fully tender, about 5 more minutes. Using an immersion blender, puree to desired consistency. Season with salt and pepper and serve.

Roasted Broccolini
with Spicy Bread Crumbs

Yield: 6 servings   **Prep time:** 20 minutes
Cook time: 20 minutes

Broccolini is broccoli's slightly bitter little sister, and it pairs wonderfully with this salty, spicy sourdough topping. Sourdough bread is a San Francisco classic, and its homemade crumbs are a tasty way to use the entire loaf. This is excellent served with a chicken dish or alongside pasta.

3 cups cubed day-old
  sourdough bread
⅔ cup freshly grated
  Parmesan cheese
1 teaspoon paprika
1 teaspoon salt, plus more
  for roasting broccolini
1 teaspoon freshly ground
  black pepper, plus more
  for roasting the broccolini
½ teaspoon cayenne pepper
4 tablespoons unsalted
  butter, melted
3 bunches broccolini
2 tablespoons extra-virgin
  olive oil

Preheat the oven to 425°F.

Place the bread in a food processor. Pulse until it reaches the consistency of crumbs. Add the Parmesan cheese, paprika, salt, black pepper, cayenne pepper, and butter and pulse a few more times to combine. Set aside.

Trim about 1 inch off the ends of the broccolini. In a large bowl, toss the broccolini in olive oil and season with salt and pepper. Place it in a single layer on a large baking sheet or roasting pan. Roast for 10 minutes, until the broccolini starts to get tender and begins to brown a little.

Cover the broccolini with the reserved bread-crumb mixture and return to the oven. Cook for another 10 minutes, until the bread crumbs are toasted. Serve hot.

Wild Rice Pilaf *with* Roasted Celery Root, Red Onions, Pine Nuts, *and* Dried Cranberries

Yield: 6 to 8 servings (7 cups)   **Prep time:** 25 minutes
Cook time: 1 hour

I first tried celery root while cooking in France, where it's a staple. It's not the prettiest vegetable, but its flavor makes it worth the effort. If you've never tried it, this root vegetable tastes like mild celery with a hint of nuttiness. The texture is creamy when it's cooked like potatoes and pureed. It's delicious with tart cranberries, pine nuts, and wild rice, which are grown all over California.

1 large celery root, peeled and cut into ½-inch dice (about 2½ cups)

1 large red onion, cut into ½-inch dice

4 tablespoons extra-virgin olive oil

Salt

3 scallions, white and green parts chopped and kept separately

1 tablespoon minced fresh ginger

2 cups wild rice, rinsed

5 cups vegetable broth

½ cup dried cranberries

¼ cup pine nuts, toasted

2 tablespoons minced fresh Italian parsley

1 tablespoon minced fresh tarragon

Preheat the oven to 425°F.

In a large bowl, toss the celery root and red onion with 2 tablespoons of the olive oil and sprinkle generously with salt. Place in a single layer on a sheet pan or baking sheet and roast until golden brown and tender, stirring once after 15 minutes, 20 to 25 minutes total.

Meanwhile, start the pilaf. In a large saucepan, heat the remaining 2 tablespoons olive oil over medium heat. Add the white parts of the scallions and the ginger and sauté just until they start to soften, about 1 minute. Add the wild rice and stir so all the rice is coated with oil. Add the broth and bring to a simmer. Turn down the heat to low, cover tightly, and cook until the rice is cooked through and the liquid is absorbed, 45 to 50 minutes. Turn off the heat, add the cranberries, stir, and cover for 5 minutes.

Remove the pilaf from the heat and stir in the roasted celery root and onions, pine nuts, parsley, and tarragon. Season with salt, garnish with the scallion greens, and serve.

Black Panther Party's Free Breakfast Program

In 1966, in Oakland, California, social and political activists and college students Huey P. Newton and Bobby Seale founded the Black Panther Party for Self-Defense. As a counterpoint to the doctrine of nonviolence practiced by Martin Luther King Jr., the Black Panther Party was an organization focused on Black self-determination, self-reliance, and taking up arms if needed to protect African Americans from the rampant police violence that plagued Black neighborhoods. Many California police officers came from the southern US and carried with them the mentality of Jim Crow and centuries of institutionalized racism. The Party quickly became one of the most influential activist groups in the nation.

Its Ten-Point Program asked for the freedom for Blacks to determine their destiny, jobs, decent housing, cultural education, military draft exemption, and an end to police brutality. One of the Party's most effective and forward-thinking efforts was the Free Breakfast for School Children program. It was part of a larger social welfare initiative that held voting drives and operated health clinics offering immunizations, sickle cell anemia screenings, and acupuncture. The Party also opened freedom schools with a culturally conscious curriculum, like the Oakland Community School, which was run by Ericka Huggins from 1973 to 1981.

The Party's free breakfast program single-handedly fed tens of thousands of kids daily through forty-five programs across the country. Children who often went to school hungry because of poverty were able to get free breakfasts of fresh oranges, eggs, meat, and chocolate milk. The effects of this program were dramatic, as teachers and school administrators reported the vast improvements they saw when well-fed children were able to focus and succeed throughout the school day.

Directed and staffed mostly by women, the Party's community survival programs provided essential services. The Panthers studied nutrition to inform breakfast choices and would barter with local grocery stores for donations. Food was cooked and served at community centers and distributed at places like the Oakland Coliseum. The Party's dedication and determination to uplifting the Black community through food transformed public schools across the nation, and its program normalized free breakfast across the country, improving the lives of American children of all races. After the Party dissolved in 1982, the US federal government began a school meal program that, in 2019, fed free or reduced-cost lunches to nearly thirty million children daily in public schools.

Congee *with* Scallions, Toasted Peanuts, *and* Virginia Ham

Yield: 6 to 8 servings (about 10 cups)   **Prep time:** 15 minutes
Cook time: 1½ hours

California is a mosaic of different cultures, and this dish melds Asian and West African traditions. Congee is a Chinese rice porridge often eaten for breakfast, but the word *congee* comes from India, where it refers to the water that the rice is cooked in. I'm paying homage to Virginia's most valuable players: peanuts and ham. And rice is right down the "road." Peanuts, also known as goobers or groundnuts, are native to West Africa, and they're found throughout Southern cuisine. Let's not forget that African-American agriculture scientist George Washington Carver invented over 300 uses for the alternative Southern crop, our favorite being peanut butter. I'm humbled to provide you with one delicious recipe. I imagine this silky porridge with smoky ham as a side dish, but top it with a fried egg and you have dinner.

1 reserved ham bone, ham hock, or ham shank
6½ cups water
4 cups chicken broth
1½ cups long-grain white rice
Salt
1 bunch scallions, white and green parts, thinly sliced
½ cup coarsely chopped roasted, salted peanuts
Roasted peanut oil (optional)

Combine the ham bone, 6 cups of the water, and broth in a large Dutch oven. Bring to a boil over high heat, lower the heat to a simmer, and cook for 30 minutes. Skim off any foam and discard.

In a fine-mesh sieve, rinse the rice several times until the water runs clear. Add the rinsed rice to the ham bone and bring to a simmer over medium-low heat. Cover and let simmer gently, stirring occasionally, until the rice is a porridge consistency, 45 minutes to 1 hour. If the mixture is getting too thick, add the remaining ½ cup water to loosen.

Once the rice has reached a porridge consistency, remove the ham bone, cut the meat off the bone, and shred it. Add all but ¼ cup of the ham to the rice and stir into the congee. Season with salt. Ladle the congee into bowls and top with the reserved ham, scallions, peanuts, and a drizzle of the roasted peanut oil if using.

Heirloom Red Beans *with* Farro *and* Poblano-Red Onion Relish

Yield: 6 to 8 servings (about 9 cups of beans)
Prep time: 30 minutes, plus 4 to 12 hours of bean soaking
Cook time: 2 hours 30 minutes

When you hear the words "red beans," you probably think "and rice." But this recipe pairing them with farro will change your mind. Farro is an ancient wheat grain that's considered a healthier alternative to rice. I love the texture it brings to this dish. This vegetarian recipe gets a meaty savory flavor and texture from the smoked paprika and the poblanos. If you're not vegetarian, pair this with your favorite sausage for a fulfilling meal.

1 pound dried red beans (I recommend Rancho Gordo Domingo Rojo)
1 tablespoon vegetable oil
1 medium yellow onion, diced small
2 stalks celery, diced small
1 small green bell pepper, cored, seeded, and diced small
3 garlic cloves, minced
2 teaspoons smoked paprika
1 tablespoon Creole spice
2 bay leaves
2 teaspoons Worcestershire sauce, preferably vegan
1 tablespoon apple cider vinegar
Louisiana-style hot sauce, to taste
6 cups water
Salt
1½ cups pearled farro

To make the beans:

Rinse the beans in cold water. In a pot, cover with water and refrigerate for at least 4 hours or up to 12 hours. Drain the beans. (If you don't have time for a soak, place the beans in a large pot and cover with water. Bring to a boil, turn off the heat, cover, let sit for 20 minutes, and drain.)

In a large Dutch oven, heat the vegetable oil over medium-high heat. Add the onion, celery, and bell pepper and cook until softened, about 6 minutes. Add the garlic and cook for 30 seconds. Add the paprika and Creole spice and stir to coat well. Add the drained beans, the bay leaves, and the Worcestershire sauce. Pour in enough water to cover the beans by 1 inch. Bring to a simmer and lower the heat to low. Cover and let simmer until the beans are tender but not falling apart, about 2 hours, stirring occasionally. If the mixture gets dry, add a little water to make it more saucy.

Once the beans are tender, season with salt; it will likely take a lot of salt. Add the apple cider vinegar and hot sauce, to taste.

continued

Heirloom Red Beans, *continued*

Poblano-Red Onion Relish:

3 fresh poblano peppers

1 tablespoon vegetable oil

½ small red onion, thinly sliced

¼ cup celery leaves

1 tablespoon red wine vinegar

Salt and freshly ground black pepper

To make the relish:

Preheat the oven to 450°F.

In a large bowl, toss the whole poblano peppers with the vegetable oil and place them on a baking sheet. Roast until their skins blister and the peppers are tender, about 15 minutes, turning halfway. Remove the peppers from the oven, place them back in the bowl, and tightly cover with plastic wrap until they are cool enough to handle, about 15 minutes.

Once the peppers are cool, peel away their blistered skins and remove the stems and seeds. Slice them into thick strips and toss with the red onion, celery leaves, and vinegar. Season with salt and black pepper. Set aside.

To make the farro:

Bring salted water to a boil in a large pot. Add the farro and boil until tender, about 15 minutes. Drain.

Spoon the farro into six bowls and top with a generous ladle of red beans. Garnish with the relish and more hot sauce.

Pimento Cheese Popovers

Yield: 12 popovers (1 cup pimento cheese)   **Prep time:** 25 minutes
Cook time: 30 minutes

If you've ever traveled down South, I hope you've enjoyed some piquant pimento cheese. Here, a mixture of sharp Cheddar cheese, cream cheese, onion, and pickled jalapeños add richness to a simple popover. The pimento cheese can be served with crackers, toasted bread, or crudités.

Pimento Cheese:

1¼ cups grated Cheddar cheese
¼ cup cream cheese
1 teaspoon hot sauce
½ teaspoon Worcestershire sauce
¼ teaspoon cayenne pepper
¼ teaspoon paprika
1 tablespoon finely chopped jalapeño chile
1 tablespoon finely chopped yellow onion
1 tablespoon minced garlic
1 tablespoon finely chopped dill pickles

3 eggs, room temperature
1½ cups whole milk, room temperature
1 teaspoon fine sea salt
1½ cups all-purpose flour

Place a wire rack in the bottom third of the oven. Preheat the oven to 450°F.

To make the pimento cheese:
In a large bowl, mix together the Cheddar cheese, cream cheese, hot sauce, Worcestershire sauce, cayenne pepper, paprika, jalapeño, onion, garlic, and dill pickles until thoroughly combined. This mixture can be made up to 1 day in advance, but it should be at room temperature when making the popovers.

To make the popovers:
Place a twelve-well muffin tin in the oven. In a bowl, whisk the eggs until well combined and lightly frothy. Add the milk and salt and whisk until the mixture is very well combined and there is a layer of froth on the top, about 30 seconds of vigorous whisking. Add the flour and whisk just until combined; it's okay if some lumps remain. Let the mixture sit for 2 to 3 minutes and then whisk one more time.

Remove the muffin tin from the oven and spray with nonstick cooking spray. Fill each muffin well three-quarters full of batter. Top each with a heaping teaspoon of the pimento cheese, and gently press the cheese down into the batter. Bake for 15 minutes, then lower the heat to 350°F and bake an additional 15 minutes, until the popovers are a deep golden brown and well puffed. Do not open the oven during this baking time.

Remove the popovers from the oven and transfer them from the muffin tin to the wire rack. Make a small hole in the bottom of each popover to allow steam to escape. Drop an additional teaspoon of pimento cheese into the top hole of each popover. These are best served immediately.

Savory Bread Pudding *with* Corn, Cheddar, *and* Thyme

Yield: 10 servings
Active time: 35 minutes   **Total Time:** 1 hour 45 minutes

I know many popular bread puddings are sweet, but this savory version is one of my favorite ways to use up all my leftovers. Bread puddings emerged as a way to revive stale bread by mixing it with ingredients that are typically in your fridge: eggs and milk.

2 tablespoons unsalted butter, plus more for greasing the pan

8 cups cubed (1 inch) good-quality, dense white bread, such as Italian or French bread (about 1 pound)

1 medium yellow onion, finely chopped (about 1½ cups)

Salt

3 cups (16 ounces) frozen sweet white corn kernels, preferably organic

4 scallions, chopped (about ½ cup)

1 garlic clove, minced

1 tablespoon sweet paprika

2 teaspoons fresh thyme

3 cups whole milk

3 cups heavy cream

4 eggs

3 cups shredded white Cheddar cheese

Freshly ground pepper

Preheat the oven to 350°F. Generously grease a 3-quart baking dish or a 9 by 13-inch baking pan with butter.

Arrange the bread cubes on a large rimmed baking sheet. Toast the cubes in the oven, stirring occasionally, until the bread is lightly golden, about 15 minutes. Remove from the oven and set aside to cool.

In a sauté pan over medium heat, melt the 2 tablespoons butter. Add the onion and 1 pinch of the salt and sauté, stirring frequently, until it turns translucent and just starts to brown, 5 to 7 minutes. Add the corn, scallions, garlic, paprika, thyme, and the remaining pinch of salt and sauté, stirring frequently, until the vegetables are warmed through and fragrant, about 5 minutes. Set aside.

In a large bowl, whisk together the milk, cream, eggs, 1 cup of the Cheddar cheese, and 1½ teaspoons salt. Then season this custard mixture with pepper.

In another large bowl, toss the vegetable mixture with the bread cubes and another 1 cup of the Cheddar cheese until well combined. Scrape this mixture into the prepared baking dish and pour the custard over it. Stir with a spoon and press down so the custard is readily absorbed by the bread and is evenly distributed. Cover with plastic wrap and refrigerate for at least 15 minutes or up to overnight.

Take the pudding out of the refrigerator and remove the wrap. Bake until the pudding turns golden brown and is set, about 45 minutes. Sprinkle with the remaining 1 cup Cheddar cheese and bake just until the cheese is melted, about 10 minutes. Let cool for 5 minutes, then serve hot.

Solomon Sweeting *of* Sweeting Ranch *in Clio*

Solomon Sweeting is proud to be living proof that you can farm almost anywhere in California. His vegetable farm and ranch is in Clio, a tiny town high in the Sierra Nevada mountains that's about seventy miles north of Truckee.

Most people know this as ski country. It snows early and often. And the white powder can blanket the ground into March. So, every year, Sweeting is racing against the elements to plant his crops early enough so he can harvest before the first fall freeze.

"You always have to be ahead of the game," Sweeting says. He gets a jump on the season by creating a tunnel or hoop house encased in plastic sheeting. Working on long tables, he germinates seeds for tomatoes, chives, and pattypan squash indoors. "You have to start things inside so that once the snow melts, you can plant your transplants."

Sweeting has acquired his farming acumen on the job; he isn't from a farming family. He's a city kid from San Francisco who never wanted to spend much time inside. "Any time I could be in nature, I'd be in nature. I've always been attracted to animals and the outdoors," he says.

He remembers admiring Black cowboys who rode the streets in the city's Ocean Beach neighborhood and seeing the Bill Pickett Rodeo, named for the famous Black cowboy who invented the rodeo sport of steer wrestling, with his mom. Sweeting started riding at the age of eight, and he later got a job grooming horses for the San Francisco Police Department. His résumé includes stints with the county agriculture department and as a wildland firefighter.

"I didn't just wake up one day and say, 'I think I'll be a poor dirt farmer,'" Sweeting says. "I like being outdoors and I like the work," he says. "If you don't like the work, you're not going to do this very long."

His farming dream really took off on the ten-acre farm he created on rented land in Loyalton. He had cattle, sheep, and horses and grew a variety of crops: corn, geraniums, chard, potatoes, mint, and fruit tree starts that people could plant. But when the owner sold that property, he had to move on.

Sweeting, his wife, and daughters returned to their property in Clio, California. It's a rustic bedroom community with million-dollar homes and seven nearby golf courses that attract visitors in the summer. That's when Sweeting's farm stand is filled with strawberries, purple orach, heirloom tomatoes, herb baskets, and flower bowls. He looks forward to chatting with customers at his little farm stand, coming up with marketing ideas, and sharing thoughts on what to make. It makes him feel good to be feeding his neighbors.

"We're in the middle of nowhere," he says. "I'm catering to my local community."

Vegan Winter Greens Stew *with* Herb Dumplings

Yield: 6 servings   **Prep time:** 25 minutes
Cook time: 45 minutes

This vegan play on chicken and dumplings is perfect for a wintry meal. The body of the stew is hearty, with bold round flavors and a slight kick from the mustard and lemon. The aromatic, airy herb dumplings are ideal for soaking up the delicious broth. It's like a comforting bowl of braised greens with extra veggies and dumplings to make it a meal.

2 tablespoons extra-virgin olive oil

6 scallions, white parts chopped and green parts sliced, kept separately

3 cloves minced garlic

¼ teaspoon cayenne pepper

½ teaspoon dried thyme

2 bunches mustard greens, thick stems removed and torn into bite-size pieces (about 10 cups)

1 large yellow onion, cut into ½-inch dice

4 carrots, peeled and cut on the diagonal into 1½-inch pieces

4 celery stalks, cut on the diagonal into 1½-inch pieces

4 cups vegetable broth

1 tablespoon molasses

1 tablespoon Dijon mustard

Juice of 1 lemon

2 tablespoons extra-virgin olive oil

Salt and freshly ground black pepper

In a large Dutch oven, heat the olive oil over medium-high heat. Add the chopped white part of the scallions, garlic, cayenne pepper, and dried thyme and cook for 30 seconds, stirring constantly. Add half of the mustard greens and stir to coat with oil; cook just until they start to wilt. Add the remaining greens, stir, and cover for 1 minute to wilt. Add the onion, carrots, celery, broth, and molasses and stir to combine. Lower the heat to medium low and let simmer until the greens and all the vegetables are tender, about 30 minutes.

Meanwhile, mix up the dumpling batter:
In a bowl, whisk together the flour, nutritional yeast, baking powder, salt, fresh thyme, oregano, parsley, black pepper, and lemon zest. Stir in the oat milk and mix just enough to form a thick dough. Let sit for 15 minutes.

When the veggies are tender, stir in the mustard and lemon juice. Season with salt and pepper. Lower the heat to a bare simmer.

continued

Vegan Winter Greens Stew *continued*

Herb Dumplings:
1¼ cups all-purpose flour
1 tablespoon nutritional yeast
2 teaspoons baking powder
1 teaspoon salt
2 teaspoons chopped fresh
   thyme
1 teaspoon chopped fresh
   oregano
1 teaspoon chopped fresh
   Italian parsley
1 teaspoon freshly ground
   black pepper
Zest of 1 lemon
½ cup oat milk

Form the dumpling dough into small balls, about 1 tablespoon of dough for each ball. Gently place the balls on top of the vegetables. Cover and cook until the dumplings have puffed up and are cooked through, 10 to 15 minutes.

Garnish with the sliced green part of the scallions and serve.

Mustard Barbecue-Roasted Quail

Yield: 4 servings   **Prep time:** 15 minutes
Cook time: 20 minutes

The small but mighty quail, which is California's state bird, will be a big hit in your house if served this way! This mustard barbecue sauce is straight out of the Carolinas, and the bourbon-soaked cherries add a fiery sweetness to balance the vinegar-based sauce. The fried sage leaves are aromatic and potato-chip crispy. You might want to fry up some extra sage leaves to nibble on while sipping with a favorite cocktail. I recommend spiking your sweet tea with a little bourbon, and don't forget the cherry.

Mustard Barbecue Sauce:
½ cup yellow mustard
1 tablespoon sherry vinegar
2 tablespoons honey
1 tablespoon Worcestershire sauce
1 teaspoon garlic powder
1 teaspoon onion powder
Salt and freshly ground pepper

8 California quail (two 1-pound packages)
2 tablespoons extra-virgin olive oil
8 fresh sage leaves

Bourbon-Soaked Cherries:
¼ cup water
¼ cup bourbon
1 tablespoon honey
¼ cup dried cherries

Preheat the oven to 500°F. Place a wire rack on a half-sheet pan. Spray the rack with nonstick cooking spray.

To make the sauce:
In a bowl, mix together the mustard, vinegar, honey, Worcestershire sauce, garlic powder, and onion powder. Season with salt and pepper.

Place the quail on the rack. Season with salt and pepper and tie their legs together with cooking twine. Reserve ¼ cup of the mustard barbecue sauce. Generously brush the remaining barbecue sauce all over the quail, inside and out. Place the quail in the oven and roast just until they're cooked through, 15 to 20 minutes.

While the quail roasts, heat the olive oil in a small sauté pan over medium-high heat. Carefully add the sage leaves (they may pop and spit a bit) and fry just until they turn crispy, about 30 seconds. Transfer from the oil to a paper towel to drain.

To make the cherries:
Combine the water, bourbon, and honey in a small saucepan over medium heat. Bring just to a simmer. Remove from the heat and add the cherries. Let soak for 5 minutes.

Remove the quail from the oven and drizzle with the reserved barbecue sauce. Top with the crispy sage leaves and sprinkle with the cherries.

Steamed Mussels *with* Fennel, Pancetta, Herbs, *and* Three Onions

Yield: 4 servings   **Prep time:** 20 minutes
Cook time: 20 minutes

Winter's abundance in California includes black mussels, golden fennel that sprouts on the side of roads and in fields, and purple, sweet, and golden onions. Fennel, pancetta, and three onions come together to create a stunning sweet and savory broth that enhances the sweet shellfish. Mussels are one of those foods that more people should cook at home: They're relatively inexpensive, delicious, and very easy to prepare. In true California spirit, serve this with a toasted chunk of sourdough bread to sop up the broth.

8 ounces diced pancetta

1 small yellow onion, thinly sliced

1 shallot, thinly sliced

1 leek, white parts thinly sliced (about 1 cup)

½ small bulb fennel, thinly sliced, plus some reserved fronds for garnishing (about 1 cup sliced fennel)

½ cup white wine

1½ cups chicken broth

2 pounds mussels, scrubbed and debearded

1 tablespoon chopped fresh chives

2 teaspoons chopped fresh thyme

2 teaspoons chopped fresh tarragon

Crusty bread for serving, like sourdough

Line a plate with paper towels. Add the pancetta to a large saucepan or Dutch oven over medium-high heat and cook until it turns crispy and brown, 5 to 7 minutes. With a slotted spoon, transfer the pancetta to the prepared plate to drain but leave the fat in the pan.

To the fat, add the onion, shallot, leek, and fennel and sauté until tender, 6 to 8 minutes. Carefully add the white wine and cook, scraping the bottom of the pan with a wooden spoon until the wine is almost completely reduced, about 3 minutes. Add the broth, mussels, chives, thyme, and tarragon. Toss to coat and cover. Steam just until the mussels open, shaking the pan occasionally, about 4 minutes. Sprinkle with the reserved pancetta and fennel fronds. Serve immediately with crusty bread.

Sweet Tea *and* Molasses–Brined Spatchcock Chicken

Yield: 4 to 6 servings   **Prep time:** 25 minutes, plus 4 to 16 hours of brining and 2 hours of chilling
Cook time: 1 hour

Sweet tea isn't just for drinking: Black tea's herbal and tannic notes, plus the citrus zest and well, sweetness, create a subtle brine for chicken. Molasses adds rich flavor and turns the bird's skin a stunning mahogany, while the tea brine leaves the meat succulent and falling off the bone. Cook up this chicken at a barbecue or in the oven for a dinner party and enjoy this quintessential Southern drink in a whole new way.

6 cups water
6 English breakfast tea bags
1 lemon, zest removed in thick strips
1 orange, zest removed in thick strips
¾ cup molasses
¼ cup granulated sugar
½ cup salt
2 cups ice
One 2½- to 3-pound whole chicken
1 tablespoon olive oil

Bring the water to a boil in a large saucepan. Remove from the heat and add the tea bags and lemon and orange zests and steep for 5 minutes. Remove the tea bags and add the molasses, sugar, and salt and stir until the molasses and salt are fully dissolved. Add the ice to cool the mixture down.

Spatchcock your chicken:
Lay your chicken, breast-side down, on a cutting board. Using sharp kitchen shears, cut along both sides of the backbone to remove it. (You will be cutting through the rib bones, so this will take a little force.) Discard or save the backbone for making stock or soup. Then flip the bird over and press hard down on the breastbone so the chicken lies flat.

Once your tea mixture has completely cooled, add the chicken, submerging it completely and letting it sit in the brine in the refrigerator for at least 4 hours or up to 16 hours.

Remove the chicken from the brine and pat it dry. Place it on a sheet pan or plate and refrigerate it for 2 hours. This will help to dry out the skin.

continued

For roasting:

Remove the chicken from the refrigerator 30 minutes before cooking.

Preheat the oven to 400°F. Place a wire rack on a half-sheet pan. Spray the rack with nonstick cooking spray.

Lay the chicken breast-side up on the rack. Drizzle with olive oil and rub to coat all the skin. You do not need to salt at this point, as the brine provides all the salt needed. Roast the chicken until an instant-read thermometer registers 160°F in the thickest part of the thigh, 45 minutes to 1 hour. Check the chicken after about 20 minutes and if the skin is getting too dark, loosely tent with aluminum foil. Remove the chicken from the oven and let it rest for at least 10 minutes before cutting it into pieces.

For grilling:

Prepare a grill for indirect grilling (for gas grills, turn one side on high heat and keep the other side off; for charcoal, place the coals on one side of the grill). Carefully oil the grill grates. Place the chicken, breast-side down, on the hot side of the grill and cook just until the skin shows grill marks, about 4 minutes. Turn the chicken over and cook the other side just until it is marked as well, another 4 minutes. Move the chicken to the cool side of grill, cover, and cook until the thickest part of the thigh registers 160°F, 25 to 30 minutes. Remove from the oven and let it rest for at least 10 minutes before cutting into pieces.

Los Angeles

The history of Los Angeles is rich with stories of Black migration, entrepreneurs, and culinary innovators. Even with its inception in 1781, the majority of the forty-four founders of L.A. were Afro-Mexicans. Enslaved Africans and Afro-Mexicans lived and labored in California before slavery was abolished in 1821. California was part of Mexico until 1847, when it was allotted to the US as part of the treaty ending the Mexican-American War.

Just before California became part of the United States, a man of partial African descent named Pío de Jesús Pico governed the land for Mexico. Pico was Afro-Mexican, and he started his career as an entrepreneur, opening a general store in San Diego. We remember him today with Pico Boulevard, which runs from one end of L.A. to the other.

By 1888, Los Angeles was home to several Black-owned restaurants and groceries. Frank Blackburn's Coffee and Chop House opened on First and Los Angeles streets, followed by Clisby and Henderson's grocery store, J. R. Walker's restaurant, and clubs like the Downbeat, Club Alabam, Apex Club, the Flame, and the Casablanca. These were centers for cultural expression, community building, and collective love for African American food and culture.

Between 1890 and 1910, a massive migration of African Americans moved to Southern California from places like Texas, Louisiana, and Georgia. Once settled in the Los Angeles area, they found blue collar jobs in industries such as construction, timber, and food service. This quickly-founded community settled in multiple areas, including one called Brick Block in downtown Los Angeles. A business district formed, mostly concentrated on Spring Street, between Eighth and Twentieth Streets, and was home to some essential African American businesses, such as the newspaper the *California Eagle*. Los Angeles had become a place that represented all the aspirations of a middle-class lifestyle: home ownership, entrepreneurial opportunities, and a chance to reinvent oneself.

Others moved to the area to build the Venice canal system. But racial discrimination in the form of restrictive land covenants meant they weren't allowed to live in Venice, so they settled in Oakwood, a 1.1-square-mile neighborhood. During the 1920s, African Americans also established a large community in Watts. These historic neighborhoods were essential for community building and economic stability.

The defense industry created countless jobs in steel, rubber, and automobile factories. In 1940, Los Angeles was home to 63,744 African Americans, and by World War II, many of South Central's established Black residents were seeking a more rural community. They looked to nearby Compton, a predominantly white area filled with farmland, chicken farms, horses, and larger houses than those in the center city. Compton offered a suburban dream for people wanting a slower lifestyle. However, the influx of Black residents was met with a series of racist real estate laws and harassment. After the Civil Rights Act of 1964 was enacted, many of these former restrictions were outlawed, and Compton became predominantly African American.

Of course, it wasn't just Los Angeles. Racism was rampant across the nation, and it influenced travel choices. The famous *Green Book*, first published in 1936 as a travel guidebook for African Americans, listed businesses like restaurants and hotels that were safe for Black travelers during the Jim Crow era. Between 1939 and 1967, the guide listed 224 Los Angeles establishments. One of the hottest was Jack's Basket Room, a popular after-hours jazz club and restaurant owned by Jack Johnson, the first Black heavyweight boxing champ. The exterior bore a famous Cab Calloway quote, "A chicken ain't nothin' but a bird." The specialty was a basket of fried chicken with shoestring fries, but they also served steaks, ham, and BBQ. A vibrant cultural scene erupted in these segregated communities. Jazz clubs such as Shepp's Playhouse, where jazz legend Charlie Parker Jr. was known to hold court, became centers of cultural pride.

Los Angeles also continued to offer economic opportunities for creative aspiring restaurateurs, and by 1970, the Black population had grown to 763,000. The 1970s brought Roscoe's House of Chicken and Waffles and Famous Amos cookies to the scene. Currently, Los Angeles is home to more than three hundred Black-owned restaurants.

Since 2005, the Taste of Soul Family Festival, a free food fair, has celebrated Black culinary excellence and creativity each October. Founder Danny J. Bakewell Sr., CEO of Bakewell Media and executive publisher of the *Los Angeles Sentinel* and *L.A. Watts Times* newspapers, launched the culinary event to showcase "all things soulful." The festival has attracted more than 350,000 attendees to Crenshaw Boulevard for everything from classic soul food dishes like fried catfish, greens, and macaroni and cheese to dishes from Africa and the diaspora.

Sorghum *and* Cinnamon-Glazed Pork Loin

Yield: 8 servings   **Prep time:** 20 minutes
Cook time: 1½ hours

I adore this pork loin recipe because of the richness of its glaze. Ancho and chipotle chiles infuse this glaze with a deep smoky flavor and give the pork a beautiful, dark, slightly caramelized crust. You'll love the way the roasted cabbage creates a silky side that's a real winner. And the best part is that both leftover make great sandwich material!

One 3-pound pork loin roast (with fat still on)
½ head red cabbage, cored and sliced into 2-inch slices
1 tablespoon vegetable oil
1 tablespoon red wine vinegar

Sorghum and Cinnamon Glaze:
2 tablespoons unsalted butter
2 garlic cloves, minced
1 shallot, minced
2 teaspoons ground cinnamon
2 teaspoons ancho chile powder
2 teaspoons pureed chipotle chile in adobo
¼ cup sorghum syrup
¾ cup chicken broth, plus more for moistening
Salt and freshly ground pepper

Preheat the oven to 375°F. Remove the pork from the fridge and allow to come to room temperature while you make the glaze.

To make the glaze:
Melt the butter in a small saucepan over medium heat. Add the garlic and shallot and sauté until translucent, about 4 minutes. Add the cinnamon and ancho chile powder and cook just until they turn fragrant, about 30 seconds. Add the chipotle chile, sorghum syrup, and ¼ cup of the chicken broth and stir and bring to a simmer. Remove from the heat, season with salt and pepper, and set aside.

Place the cabbage slices in a single layer on a sheet pan or in a roasting pan. Drizzle with the vegetable oil and vinegar, sprinkle with salt and pepper, and toss.

Pat the pork loin dry. Sprinkle it generously on all sides with salt and pepper. Place the pork loin, fat-side up, on top of the cabbage. Pour the remaining ½ cup chicken broth over the cabbage. Roast for 15 minutes. Remove from the oven, toss the cabbage, and brush the glaze generously all over the pork loin. Return to the oven and roast for 15 more minutes. Repeat tossing the cabbage and brushing the pork every 15 minutes until the pork registers 140°F on an instant-read thermometer, about 1 hour and 15 minutes total. If the cabbage starts to look dry, add a little more chicken broth to moisten. Remove the pork loin from the oven and let it rest for 15 to 30 minutes (the pork's temperature will go up another 10 to 15 degrees as it sits).

Slice the pork loin and serve with the cabbage.

North African-Spiced Oxtails

Yield: 4 to 6 servings   **Prep time:** 20 minutes
Cook time: 3 hours 15 minutes

Okay, let's be serious here: Oxtails are grown-folk food. They are the most tender, marrow-filled, and juicy meat around. Oxtail is a staple in many African-diaspora communities, especially in the Caribbean and throughout the southern United States. In this recipe, North African spices add warmth and depth to this succulent meat.

North African Spice Mix:

½ teaspoon ground allspice
½ teaspoon ground cumin
1 teaspoon freshly ground
  black pepper
½ teaspoon ground cardamom
¼ teaspoon cayenne pepper
½ teaspoon ground cinnamon
¼ teaspoon ground cloves
½ teaspoon ground coriander
¼ teaspoon ground ginger
¼ teaspoon ground mace
¼ teaspoon ground nutmeg
¾ teaspoon turmeric
¼ teaspoon dried thyme

3 to 4 pounds oxtails, fat
  trimmed to ¼ inch
2 tablespoons vegetable oil
Salt and freshly ground
  black pepper
2 yellow onions, cut into
  1-inch dice
3 stalks celery, cut into
  1-inch dice
3 large carrots, peeled and
  cut into 1-inch dice
4 peeled garlic cloves
2 cups red wine
3 cups beef broth
1 bay leaf
2 scallions, sliced,
  for garnishing

Preheat the oven to 350°F.

To make the spice mix:
Combine the allspice, cumin, black pepper, cardamom, cayenne pepper, cinnamon, cloves, coriander, ginger, mace, nutmeg, turmeric, and thyme, and mix well.

Sprinkle the oxtails generously with salt on both sides. Rub all the spice mixture all over both sides of the oxtails. Heat the vegetable oil in a large Dutch oven over medium-high heat. Sear the oxtails until golden brown on both sides, in batches if necessary, 4 to 5 minutes per side. Remove the oxtails and set aside.

Add the onions, celery, carrots, and garlic and sauté, stirring until they start to soften, about 5 minutes. Add the wine and deglaze the pan, stirring to scrape up any browned bits from the bottom of the pan. Add the beef broth and bay leaf and return the oxtails to the pan, along with any juices, nestling them into the vegetables. Bring to a simmer, then cover, and place in the oven. Braise until the meat easily pulls from the bone, 2½ to 3 hours.

Remove the oxtails from the braising liquid. Strain the liquid and discard the solids. Skim off any excess fat from the liquid and season with salt, if necessary. Serve the oxtails with the strained cooking liquid. Garnish with scallions.

Black Cowboys

It's impossible to think of the Old West without conjuring images of cowboys. But here's an interesting and little-known fact: During the 1800s, one in four cowboys were Black. Many of them were formerly enslaved and were referred to as *cowhands*.

Texas birthed Southern cowboy culture. It was colonized by Spain in the 1500s, and by the nineteenth century, cattle were central to the Texan economy. In the early 1800s, enslaved African Americans taken to Texas worked on cotton plantations and tended cattle. There were also Afro-Mexicans who had worked with cattle for generations.

In 1825, enslaved Black people made up 25 percent of the population in Texas and 30 percent by 1860. When the American Civil War broke out, Texas joined the Confederacy, and many white plantation owners joined the war, leaving their Black cowhands to tend the ranches. When the war ended, these newly freed Black cowhands demanded pay for their work, and as their profession grew, so did the references to them as cowboys. It was meant as a putdown, but by the late nineteenth century, most cowhands referred to themselves as cowboys, regardless of their racial identity.

The Black cowboys were talented cattle handlers and essential to herding the animals from state to state. These Black men and women experienced an unparalleled freedom of movement and earned respect from their white counterparts, as cowboy culture was in some ways an equalizer, even during segregation. They traveled throughout the West, from Texas to California.

Nat Love was one of these men. Born into slavery in 1854, he eventually left his home state of Tennessee at the age of sixteen and headed west. In Kansas City, he met the crew from the Duval Ranch in Texas, who had just delivered a herd of cattle. He was recruited and quickly became a respected cowboy. He worked in Arizona and Mexico, where he was called "Red River Dick." Later, in 1876, his stellar performance at a cowboy contest in Deadwood, South Dakota, earned him the nickname "Deadwood Dick." In his autobiography, Love wrote about his adventures, drinking with Billy the Kid, Pat Garrett, and other well-known Wild West characters. Love eventually retired from his cowboy lifestyle and became a Pullman porter in Colorado, settling down in Los Angeles. The nomadic lifestyle embraced by many cowboys led them to be part of the entertainment circuit as well; folks like Bill Pickett, a famous Black cowboy who invented the steer-wrestling performance called bulldogging, became part of the rodeo scene.

With the invention of barbed wire in 1867 and the establishment of America's first transcontinental railroad, the need for skilled cowboys slowly declined, but it didn't disappear. In 1922, Black businessman Nolie Murray and his wife Lela opened Murray's Dude Ranch in northern Los Angeles. This establishment was the first Black-owned vacation ranch, and its amenities included a pool, tennis courts, riding stables, and on-site housing for African Americans during segregation. Celebrities like Lena Horne and boxing champion Joe Louis were guests. It was also the set for several 1930s films, including Herbert Jeffries's all-Black westerns *Harlem on the Prairie*, *Two-Gun Man from Harlem*, *The Bronze Buckaroo*, and *Harlem Rides the Range*.

The romance of the Wild West still thrives across America, and Black cowboy culture is experiencing a renaissance. In 2021, African American photographer Kennedi Carter captured some of these scenes in her compilation entitled *Ridin' Sucka Free*, showcasing the Black men, women, and children who ride.

In California, the Oakland Black Cowboy Association has hosted a festival in West Oakland for more than forty years, and in Compton, Mayisha Akbar founded the Compton Jr. Posse in 1988 as a center for Black equestrians. In May 2020, horseback rider Brianna Noble became internationally known after she rode her horse in a Black Lives Matter protest in downtown Oakland. Her nonprofit Mulatto Meadows teaches horseback riding to people of color in the Bay Area. Through these efforts and cowboys like Anthony Harris in Compton, whose story was told in the *New York Times* in March 2018, Black cowboy culture proudly lives on

Sweet Potato Pot de Crèmes *with* Meringue *and* Spiced Candied Pecans

Yield: 6 servings   **Prep time:** 15 minutes
Cook time: 1 hour 10 minutes

Sweet potatoes are one of my favorite things to put in dessert—or anything for that matter. They are generally available fresh year-round, so you can enjoy this anytime. Far superior to its Thanksgiving rival, the pumpkin, sweet potato is a silkier, more flavorful tuber that shines with brown sugar, cinnamon, and nutmeg. This pot de crème is the perfect way to show it off in a dessert. Spiced candied pecans add crunch and give a nod to Southern pralines. You can make the meringue ahead, or even swap it for whipped cream if you're pressed for time.

1 small sweet potato
2½ cups heavy cream
¼ cup firmly packed brown
   sugar
¼ teaspoon fine sea salt
1 vanilla bean, scraped
6 egg yolks, whites reserved
   for the meringue

Meringue:
6 egg whites
½ cup firmly packed brown
   sugar
½ teaspoon cream of tartar
1 teaspoon lemon juice

Spiced Candied Pecans:
¼ cup firmly packed brown
   sugar
1 tablespoon water
½ teaspoon cinnamon
¼ teaspoon nutmeg
¾ cup pecans
1 pinch kosher salt

Preheat the oven to 300°F.

To make the sweet potato puree:
Peel and cut the sweet potatoes into large cubes and place them in a roasting pan with about ½ inch of water. Cover the pan with aluminum foil and place in a 350°F oven for about 1 hour until tender and mashable. Place in a food processor to puree.

In a saucepan, whisk ½ cup potato puree, cream, sugar, and sea salt to combine. Add the scraped vanilla bean along with the vanilla bean pod. Bring to a simmer over low heat.

Whisk together the egg yolks in a large bowl. While whisking, carefully ladle in a little bit of the hot cream mixture to "temper" the egg yolks. Continue adding the cream mixture, ladle by ladle, while whisking the whole time. Strain the mixture through a fine-mesh strainer into a spouted container, pressing with a whisk to force the liquid through. Set aside.

continued

Place six 6-ounce ramekins in a glass baking dish that is large enough to fit them all. Fill the ramekins three-quarters full with the custard. Place the baking dish in the oven and then carefully fill it with enough hot water (it does not need to be boiling) to come about three-quarters up the sides of the ramekins. Bake until the custard is set but still slightly jiggly in the center, about 35 minutes.

Remove the baking dish from the oven, being careful not to spill the hot water, and let cool to room temperature. Refrigerate the ramekins until well chilled, at least 1 hour.

To make the meringue:
Set up a double boiler on the stove. Make sure the water is only simmering, not rapidly boiling, and that it is not touching the bottom of the bowl. Add the egg whites, sugar, and cream of tartar to the bowl of the double boiler and whisk gently and continuously until the mixture is hot to the touch, or about 160°F on an instant-read thermometer, 6 to 8 minutes. You don't need to whip tons of air into the meringue at this point; you just want to gently bring the temperature up and melt the sugar. Immediately transfer the meringue to an electric mixer fitted with a whisk and beat on medium speed until it has cooled completely and is fluffy, about 10 minutes.

To make the candied pecans:
Add the sugar and water to a sauté pan over low heat and cook until the sugar is melted and bubbly. Add the cinnamon, nutmeg, and pecans and cook, stirring, until the pecans are well coated. Remove from the heat and pour the pecans onto a sheet of parchment paper or a silicone mat. Allow to cool. Once the pecans have cooled, break into pieces.

To serve, spoon a generous dollop of the meringue onto each pot de crème. Top with the candied pecans.

Brown Butter "Red Velvet" Beet Bars *with* Sour Cream Frosting

Yield: 18 bars   **Prep time:** 25 minutes
Cook time: 30 minutes

This recipe takes the traditional red velvet cake and upgrades it with nutty browned butter and sweet, earthy beets. You can add a few drops of red food coloring if you really want a rich ruby color, but the beets lend a softer hue that ranges from dark pink to warm red. The sour cream frosting is to cake what buttermilk is to pancakes: It adds that subtle acidity that heightens the sweetness.

1 cup unsalted butter
1 large or 2 small fresh red beets (about 8 ounces)
4 tablespoons distilled white vinegar
1 cup granulated sugar
½ cup firmly packed brown sugar
1 egg
1 teaspoon vanilla extract
2¾ cups all-purpose flour
1 tablespoon cocoa powder
1 teaspoon baking powder
1 teaspoon fine sea salt

Sour Cream Frosting:
½ cup unsalted butter
¼ cup full-fat sour cream
1 teaspoon vanilla extract
1 cup confectioners' sugar

Preheat the oven to 350°F. Line a 9 by 13-inch baking pan with parchment paper so the paper hangs over the sides of the pan. This will make it easy to lift the bars out of the pan once they're baked. Spray the parchment paper with nonstick cooking spray.

Place a bowl next to the stove. In a saucepan, melt the butter over low heat. Once it has melted, stir it continuously until it foams and the foam subsides, about 5 minutes. It will then foam again and slowly start to brown. Watch it closely and whisk constantly until it smells nutty and starts to turn a light brown, about 4 more minutes. As soon as it turns a rich golden brown, pour the butter into the bowl to stop the cooking. Allow the butter to cool to room temperature.

While the butter is cooling, prepare the beets. Using a paring knife (and wearing gloves so your fingers don't get discolored), peel their skins. Cut the beets into chunks and place in a food processor. Add 2 tablespoons of the vinegar and pulse until very finely chopped. Measure out ¾ cup of the beet puree.

Pour the cooled butter into the food processor. Add the reserved beet puree, the 2 remaining tablespoons of vinegar, and both the granulated and brown sugars and mix until well combined. Add the egg and vanilla and pulse until smooth.

continued

In a bowl, whisk together the flour, cocoa powder, baking powder, and sea salt. Add the flour mixture to the butter mixture in the food processor and pulse just until combined; the mixture will be thick like cookie dough. Add the dough to the prepared baking pan, pressing it in an even layer. Bake until puffed and golden brown, about 25 minutes. Remove from the heat and cool completely.

To make the frosting:
With an electric mixer, beat the butter until smooth and fluffy, scraping down the sides of the mixer with a spatula. Add the sour cream and vanilla and beat until well combined. Turn off the mixer and add ½ cup of the confectioners' sugar. Mix on low speed until well incorporated. Add the remaining ½ cup sugar and beat on low speed until combined. Raise the speed and beat until fluffy, about 30 more seconds.

Spread the frosting onto the cooled bars. Using the parchment paper, lift the bars out of the pan. Cut into eighteen squares.

Flourless Chocolate-Pecan Cake *with* Orange Glaze

Yield: One 9-inch cake, serving 8 to 12   **Prep time:** 50 minutes
Cook time: 1 hour 15 minutes

Africa is the source of so many foodstuffs that are celebrated around the world, including coffee and cocoa. Be sure to choose a fine, sustainably made baking chocolate for this recipe, since a flourless chocolate cake is all about the quality of the cacao. The orange adds a warm counterpoint that makes the chocolate taste even more exceptional.

12 ounces bittersweet chocolate (63% cacao), chopped
½ cup roasted pecan oil, plus 1½ tablespoons
2 teaspoons vanilla extract
1 cup lightly toasted pecans
7 eggs, separated
½ cup firmly packed brown sugar
2 tablespoons orange juice, plus 1 teaspoon
¼ teaspoon salt
½ cup granulated sugar

Orange Glaze:
½ cup orange juice, plus 2 tablespoons
2 tablespoons granulated sugar
Zest of 2 oranges, zested into long, thin strips with a bartender's zester
2 cups sifted confectioners' sugar
1 teaspoon vanilla extract

Preheat the oven to 325°F with a wire rack in the middle position. Generously oil a 9-inch springform pan. Line the bottom of the pan with parchment paper cut to fit.

Fill a medium saucepan with 1 inch of water; bring to a simmer. Put the chocolate in a heat-safe bowl that is large enough to fit snugly over the top of the pan without the bottom touching the simmering water. Let the chocolate melt about halfway, then remove the pan from the heat and stir the chocolate until smooth. Stir in the pecan oil. Cool slightly. Stir in the vanilla.

Grind the pecans in a blender in two batches, pulsing so you don't end up with pecan butter. (Some larger, unground pieces will remain.) Loosen the pecans from the blender with a knife, then sift them through a medium-mesh sifter into a bowl to yield ⅔ cup pecan flour (save the large bits for another use, like topping oatmeal).

Using an electric mixer with beater attachments, beat the egg yolks and brown sugar in a medium bowl until the mixture turns pale and, when the attachments are lifted, falls in thick ribbons, about 5 minutes. Beat in the orange juice (the mixture will get more liquidy). Gently fold in the ground pecans. Fold into the chocolate mixture.

In another medium bowl, using clean beater attachments, beat the egg whites with salt until foamy. Gradually add the granulated sugar and beat into soft peaks, about 10 minutes. Gently fold half of the egg whites into the chocolate mixture; then fold in the remaining whites.

Pour the batter into the prepared pan, place on the wire rack in the middle position, and bake until a toothpick inserted in the center comes out with just a few crumbs adhering, 1 to 1¼ hours. Let cool in the pan on the rack.

Meanwhile, make the glaze:
In a large saucepan, boil the orange juice, granulated sugar, and orange zest over medium-high heat until the juice is reduced by half, about 10 minutes. Using a slotted spoon, lift out the zest and transfer to a plate. Whisk the confectioners' sugar into the orange juice and pour into a spouted measuring cup. Let cool for 5 minutes, then whisk in the vanilla.

Once the cake has cooled, heat a thin metal spatula by holding it under hot water, and then dry it with a kitchen towel. Run the spatula around the inside of the springform pan, and remove the sides of the pan. Carefully trim the uneven top layer from the cake using a large bread knife. Invert the cake onto a plate. Pour half of the glaze over the cake and top with the candied orange zest.

Cut the cake with a heated knife, wiping the knife off on a hot, damp kitchen towel between slices, and serve with the remaining glaze.

Featured California
BLACK-OWNED BUSINESSES

Acta Non Verba Youth Urban Farm Project
anvfarm.org

Brown Girl Farms
browngirlfarms.com

Compton Farms USA
comptonfarmsusa.com

Freedom School Teaching Farm
fresnofreedomschool.org

Miss Oddette's Creole Kitchen
missoddettes.store

Red Bay Coffee
redbaycoffee.com

Sam Cobb Farms
samcobbfarms.com

Sweeting Ranch
facebook.com/SweetingRanch

Urban Roots Brewery & Smokehouse
urbanrootsbrewing.com

Vision Cellars
visioncellars.com

ACKNOWLEDGMENTS

It's hard to know where to start with the thank yous for this body of work. It has truly been years in the making. I am continually grateful for my mother and father for meeting in California and bringing me back to the state twice during my youth to meet extended family and enjoy the bounty of this terroir. It inspired me to buy one of my first cookbooks called California Cuisine *in 1985 and unconsciously a Chez Panisse anniversary poster to hang in my bedroom. So first of all, thank you to the state of California for constantly inspiring me.*

Thank you to my many Aunties who have always encouraged and supported me in my personal and professional life. First my pioneering great aunts who blazed the trail from Louisiana to California and Oregon: Aunt Lottie, Aunt Susan, Aunt Ruth, Aunt Emma, and Aunt Vera. To my parents' siblings and my guardian angels Aunt Maxine, Aunt Elaine, Aunt Essie, Aunt Arlene, Aunt Raye, and Aunt Mary. I've been inspired by and have learned so much from you all over the years. To my many adopted aunties: Judy, Helen, Marge, Tina, Faye . . . the list is long.

Hollis Holland—Dad . . . I don't where to begin, but I'm so glad you're still here to witness the fruits of your labor. And thanks to Bessie; my dear sister, Janelle; nieces Lyric and Marissa for keeping you on your toes!

To my long list of friends, colleagues and supporters, I can't name check you all right here, but you know who you are and I thank you, thank you, thank you!

Now for everyone who has helped bring this book to fruition. It started as an idea with literary agent extraordinaire Leslie Stoker! Leslie, I have so much gratitude for your support and guidance through this arduous process. You have made it so gratifying, and your cheerleading and championing of my work and ideas have been unparalleled.

To Alice Walker for your extraordinary words, your wisdom, kindness, and now friendship . . . I'm honored and humbled.

To Aubrie Pick for creating the most beautiful photos. You captured the spirit, essence, and soul of what I hoped to create. And you're such a joy to work with!

To my proposal and cookbook writing village:

To my proposal designer Debbie Berne, thank you for capturing my vision on such short notice with such a small budget!

To Kim Laidlaw and Janet Fletcher, I appreciate your efforts in the early versions of this project as it was starting to take shape.

The best recipe developer around, Jill Novatt. And you are so much more than that, Jill. You are a true professional, collaborator, and supporter to a scattered creative chef mind.

To Maria Hunt, I'm so thrilled that we met twenty years ago at the Foodwriters' Symposium at the Greenbrier! And now we get to enjoy that it's not just "us" in the room, but we got the party started! Thank you for your continued support, and I love that we're both in Oakland and get to meet up to toast and break bread on a whim.

To Dr. Kelley Fanto-Deetz, I can't believe the chance introduction I had to you and your work. Your enthusiasm for your subject expertise is infectious. Thank you for your work!

To Editor-in-Chief Lorena Jones, thank you for your belief in me and my work and for your generous support of this book. It means so much after all these years in this industry.

To editor and art director Emma Rudolph and Emma Campion. The Emmas! You have both been a pleasure to work with and though mostly over zoom, we got it done! And thank you to Kim Keller for pulling up the reins in the end.

To the design team Sebit Min, Annie Marino, and Mari Gill, for creating such a beautiful book. And thanks to Jane Chinn for managing production.

To my Dream team for looks and my soul sisters: Grace Coliandres and Nyanda Lightheart.

To my Dr. Shirley Everett and Eric Montell at Stanford Residential Dining Services, thank you for letting me bring some flavors to Stanford University!

Leslie Quiocho and Donald King at Good Eating Company for embracing my vision of bringing California Soul to a broader audience.

Kathryn Porter for welcoming me to Oakland and later for welcoming me to Booneville over and over again.

Lynell Green and Glen Sherman for unconditional business support. Okay, maybe there were a few conditions, but only we know!

Brown Sugar Kitchen, B-Side, and Town Fare staff over the years. There are so many layers between visionary, leader, manager, and boss . . . . I hope you see this one day.

To all of the wonderful women chefs cooking in California who inspire me daily. Especially my local Bay Area go-tos: Alice Waters, Dominica Rice, Romney Steele, Yang Peng, Gayle Pririe, Kim Alter, Dominique Crenn . . . you are colleagues, friends, and inspiration!

INDEX

Typefaces: Monotype's Plantin MT and Klim Type Foundry's Founders Grotesk

Library of Congress Cataloging-in-Publication Data
Names: Holland, Tanya, author. | Deetz, Kelley Fanto, author. |
    Hunt, Maria C., author. | Pick, Aubrie, photographer.
Title: Tanya Holland's California soul : recipes from a culinary journey West /
    Tanya Holland with Dr. Kelley Fanto Deetz and Maria C. Hunt; photographs
    by Aubrie Pick.
Description: First edition. | New York : Ten Speed Press, [2022] |
    Includes index.
Identifiers: LCCN 2022005493 (print) | LCCN 2022005494 (ebook) |
    ISBN 9781984860729 (hardcover) | ISBN 9781984860736 (ebook)
Subjects: LCSH: African American cooking. | Seasonal cooking—California. |
    Cooking, American—Southern style. | LCGFT: Cookbooks.
Classification: LCC TX715.2.A47 H65 2022 (print) | LCC TX715.2.A47 (ebook) |
    DDC 641.59/296073—dc23/eng/20220225
LC record available at https://lccn.loc.gov/2022005493
LC ebook record available at https://lccn.loc.gov/2022005494

Hardcover ISBN: 978-1-9848-6072-9
eBook ISBN: 978-1-9848-6073-6

Printed in China

Editor: Emma Rudolph | Production editor: Kim Keller
Designer: Sebit Min | Art director: Emma Campion |
    Production designers: Annie Marino, Mari Gill, and Mara Gendell
Production and prepress manager: Jane Chinn
Food stylist: Carrie Purcell
Prop stylist: Claire Mack
Copyeditor: Mi Ae Lipe | Proofreader: Adaobi Obi Tulton |
    Indexer: Elizabeth Parson
Publicist: David Hawk | Marketer: Samantha Simon

10 9 8 7 6 5 4 3 2 1

First Edition

Tanya Holland's inventive cuisine—rooted in a Black Southern cultural repertoire with a twenty-first-century sensibility using local, sustainable, chef-driven, seasonal ingredients—is showcased in recipes for every season, such as Collard Green Tabbouleh, Zucchini–Scallion Waffles with Toasted Pecan Romesco, Grilled Shrimp and Corn with Avocado White Barbecue Sauce, Fried Chicken Paillards with Arugula and Pea Shoot Salad, Fig and Almond Crostatas, and Honey Lavender Chess Pie.

The recipes—influenced by the Great Migration of African American families, including Tanya's own—reveal the key ingredients, techniques, and traditions that African Americans brought with them as they left the South for California, creating a beloved version of soul food. Beyond the recipes, Tanya spotlights ten contemporary Black Californian foodmakers—farmers, coffee roasters, and other talented artisans—whose work defines California soul food, with stunning portraiture and stories. Filtered through the rich history of African American migration that brought her own family from the Deep South to the West Coast, Tanya's recipes are as comforting and delicious as they are steeped in history.